COMMERCIAL REAL ESTATE:
EVERY QUESTION ANSWERED

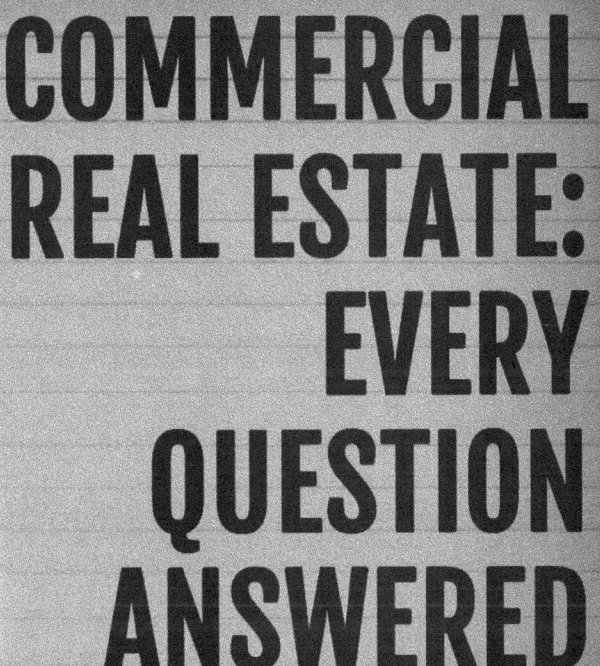

COMMERCIAL REAL ESTATE: EVERY QUESTION ANSWERED

A COLLECTION OF QUESTIONS ASKED BY THOSE LOOKING FOR ANSWERS TO THE GREAT MYSTERY OF COMMERCIAL REAL ESTATE

BY DANIEL P. KRUSE

COMMERCIAL REAL ESTATE BROKER AND EXPERT IN POSITIONING REAL PROPERTY ASSETS FOR SALE AND LEASE

Publisher: Daniel P. Kruse/Long Time Press

Cover Design and Photography: Daniel P. Kruse

Title Page and Author Photos: G. Bokeh and Daniel P. Kruse

Author: Daniel P. Kruse

Illustrator: Marty Bucella

ISBN: 979-8-9882100-1-6 (hardcover)

ISBN: 979-8-9882100-0-9 (paperback)

ISBN: 979-8-9882100-2-3 (eBook)

Library of Congress Control Number: 2023907552

This publication is designed to provide accurate and authoritative information in regard to the subject matter covered. It is sold and distributed with the understanding that the publisher is not engaged in rendering legal, accounting, or other professional services. If legal advice or other expert assistance is required, the services of a competent professional person should be sought.

Printed in the United States of America.

Author & Publisher Information: **www.DanielPKruse.com**

To my daughters, Perri and Rachel,
who always seem to have an
endless supply of questions.

Keep asking.

CONTENTS

Chapter One (For Sellers):

I Am an Owner Who Wants to Sell My Property   1

Finding and hiring a broker, commissions, marketing, cleanup of your property, hazardous waste, escrow, contingency period, closing the sale, and tax deferred exchanges

Chapter Two (For Buyers):

I Am a Buyer Who Wants to Purchase a Property   51

The first thing a buyer should do, what to consider, where to buy, how to buy, building size, bidding wars, financing your deal, the SBA, walk-through inspections, title reports, and when to close an escrow

Chapter Three (For Landlords):

I Am an Owner Who Wants to Lease My Property   93

The first thing a landlord should do, using a broker, how brokers are paid, proper marketing, broker vs. attorney, number of real estate agents you need, building improvements that increase lease rates, types of tenants, and getting the highest lease rate

Chapter Four (For Tenants):

I Am a User Who Wants to Lease a Property

Where to start, planning a move, lease vs. purchase, electricity and equipment, submitting an offer, zoning and conditional use permits, insurance, options, and subleasing

PREFACE

This is a book of questions . . . questions I have been asked over the course of my real estate brokerage career. I wanted to take the knowledge I acquired in thirty-plus years as a broker and share it with others by compiling these questions, along with their answers, in one place; this book is the result. But how long and detailed should my answers be? I thought about this, and the following came to me:

In my seventh-grade English class, we were given an assignment to answer questions about a classic American novel we had been reading (or were supposed to have read). My hand shot up, and I asked our teacher, Mr. Fox, how long our answers should be. He always reminded me of Dean Martin with his voice, swagger, and sense of humor, and I can remember his answer to this day: he looked me square in the eye and said, "As long as a dog's legs." My classmates and I were a little perplexed for a few seconds until Mr. Fox explained by asking and answering his own question:

"How long is a dog's leg? Long enough to reach the ground."

In other words, the answer can be long or short, depending on whether the response fully answers the question. So, the answers to the questions in this book will be as long as a greyhound's legs or as short as a dachshund's, just as long as they get the job done.

Some of my answers could be shorter, and almost all of them could be much longer if they included examples and went off on tangents, but I did not want to turn this into a law book.

All of my answers are complete, but if you are looking for a more detailed and in-depth explanation of a particular question or special situation, I suggest you contact a highly specialized and respected real estate attorney or a CPA specializing in commercial real estate. If you want realistic and real-world answers from someone who is in the trenches on a daily basis, you have come to the right place.

In my practice of consulting, marketing, selling, and leasing commercial real estate, I do not simply sit in a corner office charging my clients for every fifteen minutes of conversation or attention I give to their situation. I am mostly on the move, meeting building owners, inspecting the amenities of a building, climbing onto a roof, driving my car to the next meeting while talking to a client on the phone (hands-free, of course), or negotiating with an opposing agent to complete a transaction.

I sincerely enjoy helping the people I meet resolve their problems by finding solutions to their special situations. My goal? To ensure commercial real estate remains an uncomplicated asset instead of a difficult and demanding liability.

My commercial real estate career, along with this book you are holding, will be as long as a dog's leg: long enough to get the job done.

Enjoy!

—Dan Kruse, 2022–2023

INTRODUCTION

I have encountered many interesting and colorful owners throughout my years as a commercial real estate agent. Some didn't care who they hired, but most were very particular about who they chose to represent their best interests, get the highest price, and get the job done as professionally and quickly as possible.

One day, during my very first year in the business, perhaps even the first month, I was walking the streets, literally knocking on the doors of commercial buildings trying to speak to anyone. I was asking if they wanted to buy, sell, or lease a building—or if they had *any* kind of real estate requirement that I could help them with. This is known as cold-calling, and I didn't like it. I know very few people who do . . . and I don't believe those few who claim they do are telling the truth.

I doubt if anyone I encountered that day really wanted to talk real estate or ask the advice of a twenty-two-year-old kid, fresh out of college. But they say it's a numbers game, and I guess my number came up that day in the form of an older, eccentric widow whom I will call Mrs. H. She owned two industrial buildings side by side. Both buildings were filled with all sorts of items. I guess these days, we call this hoarding. Mrs. H and I struck up a long conversation that day about all sorts of things. Every so often, we would talk about her two buildings, which she thought were worth twice as much as any other building.

Mrs. H kept reminding me that in all her years, she had never used a real estate broker and didn't really like them. I mostly nodded in agreement and laughed where appropriate in an effort to build a rapport, always trying to steer her back to deciding what she wanted to do with her two "valuable" buildings. Eventually, she told me to come back tomorrow, and she would list them with me for lease. So, the next day, I returned, and we spoke again, rehashing almost word for word what we had talked about the day before. This went on for four days. By the fifth day, I was worn out, but I got the listing.

Just two days later, I spoke to an older man I will call Mr. A, who also owned two large industrial buildings side by side on the same street as Mrs. H. Mr. A was always working on some kind of project or carrying out maintenance on his property . . . never really getting anything done but keeping himself busy rattling around his large, empty buildings. Like Mrs. H, Mr. A made it clear he had never liked or used real estate brokers either. After several days of engaging in weird, disjointed conversations with Mr. A, he, too, finally gave me a listing to sell or lease his buildings.

How about that? In less than two weeks, I listed four buildings belonging to owners who not only did not like real estate brokers but also had never hired them!

Following this success, I decided to cold-call the other side of the street, mainly because a small commercial building that looked like it had been abandoned for ages caught my eye. I researched the owner and discovered that he was located at a business just down the street. So, I walked over and asked to see Mr. M. Mr. M told me he hadn't given much thought to his old building, but he asked me a lot of questions, some having to do with real estate, some not. He told me to come back the next day to discuss it further.

The next day, I went back for nothing more than conversation. On the third day, I returned, and Mr. M told me he wanted me to sell the old building. He gave me the keys to the front door and told me to walk through the building and give him my opinion of its value. I drove down the street, pulled up in front of the building, got out of my car, and unlocked the front door. The building was constructed from a combination of concrete blocks, frame and stucco, and dirt from a small hill. Yes, one of the rear walls was not even a wall; it was hardened dirt from the embankment of a freeway overpass. After walking through the building, I returned and gave Mr. M my thoughts, none of which were too favorable. He looked me in the eye and said, "Sell it."

In a span of about three weeks, I was able to obtain three listings consisting of five buildings on the same street. That "street" was the frontage road to the Santa Ana Freeway (Interstate 5) at Katella Avenue, near Disneyland in Anaheim. I ordered five of the largest real estate signs available and mounted them on each of the five roofs. It was impossible to drive along the freeway through Anaheim and not see my name. No one, not even Disneyland, had better freeway signage than I did. During the first three weeks, I received fifteen to twenty calls per day. Yes, per day. My career took off with a bang.

It wasn't long before I was receiving calls from other brokers asking me how I had gotten the listings. Several who were more experienced than I was, told me they had spoken to these owners many times but had come up empty.

My chats with Mrs. H, Mr. A, and Mr. M had morphed into an interview of sorts. None of them liked real estate brokers, maybe because no previous broker had ever taken the time to make them feel comfortable about working with one. In fact, most of the real estate questions Mrs. H, Mr. A, and Mr. M asked me were not very complicated, perhaps intentionally. Looking back, I realize they were probably sizing me up, seeing what I was made of, or maybe they just wanted to give a kid a break.

As I became older and wiser, I was asked more involved and complicated questions. These questions were not necessarily more involved and complicated for me but for the owner. I did not know the answer to every question, but in those cases, I looked to experts in a particular field who could provide the best answer and complement my team for the client's benefit.

I enjoy going into a meeting with an owner who has a whole slew of questions as they try to figure out what to do with what is likely their greatest and most valuable asset. I will always detail all sides of the situation so we can strategize and discuss their best course of action. Sometimes this means they do not require my services. While this is disappointing, what is of the utmost importance is the client and whatever is in the client's best financial interests, not mine.

Nine times out of ten, those clients or their friends and family will contact me, sometimes years later, even if we have never completed a transaction together. Why? Because they remember that I gave them accurate, thorough information and advice before, and they know I will do it again.

What follows are questions clients have asked me countless times in my more than thirty-year career. Now you can have the benefit of these answers. Hopefully, this book will answer your questions too. If it only prompts more questions, call me. I'm in the book!

HOW TO USE THIS BOOK

Any time I see a section titled "How to Use This Book," I think, "Really? You pick up a book and just start reading, don't you?" But the more deeply I got into writing this book, the more I could see that if you did not have day-to-day experience working in commercial real estate, there might be items or phrases that would be unfamiliar. Just like when you play a board game for the first time, there are instructions and rules you need to understand to play the game correctly. So, if there are any rules or instruction pages for this book, here they are. These are the things you should familiarize yourself with and remember while reading this book.

No matter what business you are in, there are certain words or phrases you and your coworkers know and use that others outside that business may not know or use in the same way. In the restaurant business, a server might say, "I need two cows. Make them cry, and make one a hockey puck." That server just told the cook to make two hamburgers with onions, and one of them should be well done. Those on the inside of a business have a slightly different way of saying the same thing than those on the outside.

For example, when my fellow brokers (who might actually be agents) use the word "broker," they might actually mean "agent." It's important to know that when the word "broker" is used in this context, it's meant to describe a person working in real estate, not an actual brokerage house business.

We use the following terms interchangeably in the commercial real estate brokerage business, even though there is a specific definition for each that makes them quite different.

Broker = Agent

Commercial Real Estate Broker = Agent

Agent = Agent (that was a joke)

Lease = Rent

Tenant = Lessee = Renter

Landlord = Lessor = Owner

Guarantee = Guaranty

Property = Facility = Building = Subject

Lease Rate = Rental Rate

His = Hers, Him = Her, She = He

Also note that although this book is about commercial real estate on the whole, it most closely addresses industrial property. While there are certain aspects that retail, office, and investment real estate do not necessarily share with industrial real estate, what is contained in this book can apply to retail, office, and investment real estate as well.

Throughout this book, you will encounter answers and stories that mention a lease rate or a sale price. These rates may seem inexpensive to you while you are reading this. The actual prices are not as important as what the example or story illustrates, and if the prices are lower than they are while you are reading this, it just reinforces the fact that real estate is a good investment.

The answers and discussions throughout this book are based upon California law.

Each chapter will have the following categories: **Starting Out** (some of the first things you need to do or consider), **Improvements** (actual fixtures, enhancements, or additions to the property), **Strategy** (ideas, tactics, or thoughts to help buy, sell, or lease property, etc.), **Fine-Tuning** (altering, modifying, or revising the plan), and **Closing** (doing that last-minute thing to conclude the sale or lease). This will give you an idea of where in the book the questions and answers might fall depending on where you are in the buying, selling, or leasing process—or whatever you are trying to accomplish.

Lastly, if you are not quite sure of the meaning of a word or phrase, I have included a short glossary of terms at the end of this book. Are you ready? Here we go.

CHAPTER **1** ONE

"You are only as good as the benefit you impart to others."

— Daniel Kruse

I Am an Owner Who Wants to Sell My Property

Okay, so you are the owner of an industrial building. Maybe you operated your business in the building, or maybe you have owned it for fifteen years and have had only one tenant during that time. Maybe you just inherited it and don't know what to do next, or maybe you are tired of managing the property. Whatever your reason for selling, your wisest course of action is to gather all of the best information possible because you only get to sell your building once. So, you'd better make it good!

For reasons that will become evident as you read further, the absolute best way to maximize your asset and obtain the highest price possible is to use the valuable information and knowledge of a commercial real estate broker. But not just ANY commercial real estate broker. Get the best. You and your property deserve it. You can pay a real estate commission and get an average (or even below average) agent or pay the same amount and get the best possible service from a real estate broker in your area who is just right for you and your property.

Let's start building our knowledge by getting your questions and concerns answered. But let's also have some fun.

Question: Should I use an agent to sell my property?

Answer: You don't really need to know everything about selling your real estate if you hire a real estate professional who does. As Steve Jobs once said, "It doesn't make sense to hire smart people and then tell them what to do; we hire smart people so they can tell us what to do." By hiring a professional commercial real estate broker, you will have someone in your corner who has a great deal of education and experience in the neighborhood in which your property is located. A seasoned agent offers other benefits too. A broker who has twenty-plus years of experience is going to have much deeper knowledge than someone who was licensed six months ago. That translates into a better value for the client. You want a broker who will present you with the right information at the right time so you can make an informed decision.

Agents have intimate knowledge about your property's surrounding area and can identify comparable sale transactions that are of consequence and meaning. Without an agent, you can go down to the county records office and find out what a property has sold for, but rarely will you know how it sold, why it sold, and the backstory that can really tell the true story of a transaction. Professional real estate agents know the market conditions in your area and have an entire network of other agents they have done business with in the past. They have the inside scoop and are able to get the real dirt on how and why a transaction occurred.

Hiring a real estate agent will get your property in the various multiple listing services that are so valuable in today's marketplace. Also, by using a professional real estate agent, you will receive guidance on the latest rules, regulations, and laws regarding commercial property sales.

A professional real estate agent has negotiation skills, one of which is the ability to remove themselves from the emotional aspects of a transaction. They are also obligated to hold client information confidential from competing interests.

When you receive an offer, your agent will help you decide whether you should accept it or submit a counteroffer. Your agent will negotiate a better deal and help you navigate the appraisal, title, and inspection process. They will also help you get through the mountain of paperwork that you will encounter during the transaction.

An experienced broker will help you price your property right for the current market conditions, saving you hours of research time. A common mistake sellers can make is pricing their property too high—or worse, too low. Brokerage firms keep up with the current industry and economic trends, as well as any significant recent sales in their area of operation. They will use sales comps analysis to determine a fair but realistic listing price for your building but will allow room for negotiation with potential buyers.

Seasoned commercial real estate brokers have a well-established professional network of other brokers, investors, and additional third parties who may be interested in purchasing your commercial real estate right away. Rather than relying solely on traditional marketing strategies, your broker can present your property directly to these individuals, significantly increasing your chances of finding a qualified buyer quickly.

Brokers have created connections after years—even decades—in the business. Their connections alone make hiring an experienced broker a good choice.

True Story

When I sold my own home, even though I was a commercial real estate broker, I thought I would hire a residential real estate broker since they knew the area and had experience in residential real estate. Despite having many more years of experience selling real estate than any of the residential brokers I interviewed, I wanted the expertise of a knowledgeable residential agent.

I tried calling the "top" agent in the area, but his assistant told me he was booked and could only call me back in about a week. I declined. Instead, I found and interviewed three different brokers and asked each of them how they could get me the highest possible price for my home.

The answers I received and the information I was given were underwhelming. One agent spent almost forty-five minutes telling me how wonderful he was, never once asking me about *what I wanted*. Another agent regurgitated the company's marketing material. The third agent spoke almost exclusively about the importance of having the right forms. He made it his mission to make sure I knew that he had the right forms and knew how to fill them out the right way.

I don't need more than a basic five-minute biography on an agent, I can read company literature myself, and I can wade through paperwork myself. I wanted someone who could *add value* to the transaction and maximize my asset so I would receive as much from the sale as possible—certainly more than if I did not use a broker.

I sincerely could not place the sale of my home in the hands of any of the three agents I had interviewed. I called the "top" agent again, but just as before, he could not return my call for at least a week. I finally decided to take a week off of work to study the neighborhood, obtain the comps, try to see what progress I could make, and seriously consider listing my property myself.

I did all the marketing for my house that a residential agent would do, including listing it on the multiple listing service (this is something the typical homeowner cannot do unless the homeowner is a licensed real estate broker).

True Story continues . . .

True Story continued . . .

Once it became common knowledge that my home was listed, that "top" agent who was too busy to call me back suddenly called me up wanting to list the property. I kindly said that I would think about it and call him in a week.

I sold the property myself for the full asking price in nine days using a method that I have never seen a residential agent use. No, I won't tell you here.

I am not telling you to try to complete residential real estate transactions or commercial real estate transactions on your own. Quite the contrary. If I had not had a thorough background in real estate, I would not have attempted to sell my own property.

The moral of the story? Find an agent who asks you what *you* want—someone who can add real monetary value to the transaction; has a custom, creative marketing plan; and can return a phone call in less than a week.

Question: How do I find a commercial real estate broker?

Answer: There are many steps to take to locate a worthy commercial real estate broker. If you have been receiving periodic mailers regarding your commercial property or have been receiving phone calls from one or two commercial real estate agents, that is one of the first places to begin. Obviously, these real estate agents are interested in your property and probably work in the area where your property is located, so they would be one of the richest sources of information.

Another way to locate a real estate broker would be to drive around the neighborhood in which your commercial property is located and look for real estate signs. This would give you an indication of which companies and agents work in and around the area of your commercial property.

You could also do a Google search for commercial real estate in the city in which your facility is located, which would also give you a very good idea of which brokers and agents work in your area.

Question: How do I hire a commercial real estate broker?

Answer: You should interview *at least* two commercial real estate brokers in order to get a good indication of who you would be comfortable working with. If you have the time and patience to interview three agents, that will give you an even more well-rounded view of the market and how your property fits into the current marketplace.

Some of the questions you might want to ask are how long the agent has been in the business, which similar properties they have sold or leased, what they think your property is worth, how long they think it will take to sell or lease, etc. Take notes; you won't remember all of their answers.

It's also important to obtain a written package or proposal from each real estate broker to see whether it's tailor-made for you and your needs or if it is a generic proposal their computer spat out earlier that day. This is a good indicator of what efforts and steps each agent will take on your behalf.

Question: What are the top five questions I should ask a real estate broker when interviewing them for a listing?

Answer: What type of real estate do you sell—and in what market? Why should I hire you? How many transactions have you done in an area with property similar to mine? What is my building worth and why? What is your experience, and do you represent any other similar properties right now? These are must-ask questions. Okay, now you are on a roll. Keep the questions coming.

Question: Why should I pay a commission to a real estate agent when I can lease or sell my building myself and not pay the commission?

Answer: Even if you, as an owner, don't ask this question, it's always in the back of your mind when you have a property to sell or lease. This is the age-old question, and it comes up time after time. Think about this: professional property owners who buy and sell commercial property as their primary business should know more about real estate than the average commercial property owner, yet these professionals, more often than not, employ a commercial real estate broker to sell or lease their property. Why is this? Perhaps I can best illustrate this with a true story from my own personal experience.

True Story

I once sat in the office of a husband and wife who wanted to sell their industrial building. It was the only other real estate they owned besides their home. They had operated their business out of the building for more than twenty years, but now they were retiring. This property would make up the largest portion of their retirement income, so they were counting on every penny. They asked me why they should pay a 6% commission when they could sell it themselves and put the commission they would have paid toward their retirement.

I asked them what their asking sales price would be if they sold it themselves. They had done a lot of research, talked to a real estate agent and fellow building owners, and felt confident that the market price for their building was around $150 per square foot. In fact, they had received an offer and were seriously thinking of accepting it.

I told them that if they hired me, I could potentially get them well in excess of $150 per square foot. There were also many other issues that I wanted them to be aware of, such as the fact that the property needed a Phase 1 and possibly a Phase 2 environmental study. There was a lot of functional obsolescence that needed addressing, repairs that many buyers would want done, and problems with the title report that would need some cleaning up. There were also many contingencies that the owners would have to face on their own without the knowledge and expertise of someone who had dealt with them many times before.

The more I spoke the facts and truth to them, the more intently they listened to me (especially the part about me being able to obtain a higher sales price). They finally agreed to award me the listing for a two-week period. Shortly after, I was able to bring them a buyer for $185 per square foot. The extra $35 per square foot more than paid for my commission and brought the sellers almost 300,000 additional dollars for their retirement that they had not counted on.

They later confided in me that they had settled on selling their building to a neighbor for $145 per square foot. This could have been a disaster for them financially. I'm glad they trusted me to help them.

As you can see, in many cases, having a qualified, experienced, and knowledgeable real estate broker on your side is worth more than a mere commission.

I always try to bring added value to a transaction. So, I am constantly striving not only to earn my commission but also to exceed the owner's expectations. There are other similarly thinking brokers; you just need to find one.

Question: Besides the commission, what other expenses am I responsible for as a seller?

Answer: As a seller, you will be responsible for half of the escrow fees. Escrow fees are usually determined by the total purchase price of a property. You will also be responsible for the cost of a title report. No buyer will want to purchase a property unless it has a free and clear title. This is insured by a title company. A title company will insure you for any item that does not show on a title report. These items could be a judgment, a lien, unpaid taxes, and any other cloud on the title. Again, generally, the cost for the title insurance is directly linked to the total purchase price of the property. There are other miscellaneous costs as well, including staging the property.

Question: We are concerned about having only one agent on the listing instead of a team of two or three. Isn't it true that the more agents you have working on a listing, the more territory they can cover?

Answer: Having two or three agents on a listing can seem like a good idea at the outset, and it is a good idea if you are leasing a commercial park with buildings of differing sizes, such as multi-tenant, mid-size, and large facilities. Two or three agents might also be helpful if you are leasing a mixed-use park, such as retail, office, and industrial units. However, read on. I am about to pull the curtain back . . . just a little.

A "team" usually consists of a senior agent, brought in to show the owner experience and dealmaking ability, and less senior agents who do most or all of the work. Team members often think the other guy is "doing it" or the other guy "will do it," and consequently, less gets done. So, what the owner sees is often not what they really get.

With so many team members involved from the start, the natural inclination is to try to find a buyer without involving an outside broker, thereby obtaining twice the fee for selling the property. But this can only hurt the owner because a lack of timely and aggressive marketing to outside agents means less exposure to possible buyers.

With two or three agents involved, personalities can clash, and a lack of accountability can occur, as well as scheduling conflicts, a dilution of reward for work, and resentment because one member is overworked, and another is underworked. Additionally, there may be a lack of consensus regarding marketing, negotiations, and sale documentation.

With one agent involved, there is a greater focus on the project, no personalities to conflict with one another, a higher reward for effort, no scheduling conflicts, and more accountability.

Question: This is a significant portion of our portfolio, and we are concerned about choosing a broker who will be sincerely concerned for our welfare and our benefit from the ultimate transaction. What do we do to make sure the broker we choose understands this?

Answer: A broker demonstrates their sincerity to your project by not working on any other competing property during the active marketing of yours. You want an agent to work on your project with the same understanding of your property that you have.

By hiring a broker, you are putting your real estate and financial matters in the hands of someone else and giving up some degree of control. Even if you know you might need outside expertise, it is emotionally discomforting to put your affairs in someone else's hands. A broker should do everything possible to help you eliminate, or at least reduce, your apprehension. Regularly scheduled meetings or phone calls between you and your broker can help relieve that anxiety.

Question: If I hire a real estate agent, do I need a CPA or an attorney?

Answer: I would highly recommend you hire a certified public accountant (CPA) in all cases and engage a real estate attorney for a few hours in order to facilitate the smoothest, least taxing, and most lawsuit-free transaction possible.

In reality, I have done hundreds of transactions, and the majority have been done without the assistance of a CPA or an attorney. However, as tax laws become more complex and people become more and more litigious, it is important to know every aspect of what is happening to prevent any surprises.

The sale or purchase of a commercial property is not like buying a pair of pants. It happens very infrequently. So, it's best to have the brightest and most respected professional representation in your corner. It's also always a good idea to double-check or triple-check what you think is accurate and get a second or third opinion when the stakes are so high.

For example, if you were selling a $2.5 million property and had to sit down with a CPA who cost you $300 an hour and an attorney who cost you $400 an hour for five hours each, it would only cost $3,500. This is less than a fifth of a percent of the entire purchase price—a great bargain to ensure you're doing the right thing.

Question: How long should I list with a real estate broker?

Answer: This may depend on what kind of relationship you have with your real estate broker, the type of property you have to list, and how brisk or slow the real estate market is.

If you are just getting to know your real estate broker and want to "test" them out, you might opt for a short-term listing in case a reason develops to end the relationship.

I would *not* recommend granting a listing for more than three months. If things are going well, and you feel your real estate broker is servicing the listing, you can always renew the listing for an additional period.

In my experience, agents with six-month listings tend to be a little lazy, and they don't give a listing their full attention during the first few weeks of the listing period, possibly because they feel they have control of that property for the next six months. If you give an agent a listing for a shorter period, they tend to be more motivated to accomplish your goals.

I have personally taken listings for a much shorter period in an effort to prove to the owner that hiring me was an excellent choice. Talk about motivation! When you have a ten-day listing, you make sure every day counts. I did this and won the trust of the owner, and in three weeks, I brought him a tenant whom he has had for more than ten years. However, I would not recommend this practice to either an owner or a broker unless there was a special case or circumstance that made this type of arrangement necessary.

In summary, give the real estate broker a reasonable time period to act on a listing, but do not be afraid to shorten it if you are not happy with their performance.

Question: How can I be sure that the agent I hire is working to sell _my_ building, especially if the agent has other listings?

Answer: I think it is important to have particular milestones, especially when you begin marketing and selling the property. There should be constant communication between the seller and the seller's broker at each specific interval of the marketing process.

Have the broker call you when the property has been listed on multiple listing services, when a brochure and floor plan are published, when the "For Sale" sign is installed on the property, and _each time_ the property is shown to potential buyers. Most importantly, have the broker inform you of the results of each showing.

When the broker knows that you want to be involved at each stage, you will have a much more engaged, involved, and attentive broker on your side.

The worst call any real estate broker can receive is from the building owner asking, "What's happening with my building?" If you have to ask that question, you might want to prepare yourself for some heavy tap dancing from your broker.

"The building owner said he only wants one sign."

Question: Can I sell my building without placing a "For Sale" sign on it?

Answer: If you have a real estate broker who is well known by their fellow agents, property owners, and others who frequent the area in which your property is located, you do not need a "For Sale" sign.

What are some of the reasons you would not want a "For Sale" sign on the building? Maybe you, as the owner/seller, have your own business in the building and do not want your competitors or your customers to know you are selling the building. Or the building might be vacant, and you believe having a "For Sale" sign on the property will attract vandalism. Whatever the case may be, an active real estate broker does not need to place a sign on the property to conduct an effective marketing campaign. If you have chosen your real estate agent well, your agent knows that there are many other ways to attract a buyer to a property than a mere sign.

I completed an informal study surveying many brokers, asking them how they obtained a buyer or a tenant and if the buyer or tenant was attracted to the property because of the sign. Out of almost 150 transactions, only about 18% of the deals transacted were specifically because of a sign installed on the property. That being said, if you want to create the most interest in a property and increase the motivation of those who are interested, the proper placement of a "For Sale" sign is important.

One of the best reasons to have a sign is to assist cooperating brokers when they drive their clients to see a property. It can help the agent quickly identify the building.

Quick Thought: If your building is located off of a main street with heavy traffic, and you prefer to have signs to advertise its availability, see if your broker can place a sign on that heavy-traffic intersection with an arrow and a rider on the sign with the address of your building. It's a great way to increase the interest in your building.

Question: Does a "For Sale" sign help?

Answer: In a survey I personally conducted some years ago and an identical survey that was done a few years later, the percentage of commercial property buyers attracted to a property after seeing a "For Sale" sign was 18%.

Does this mean "For Sale" or "Available" signs are a waste of time? That depends. There are pros and cons to having a "For Sale" sign on a property. Personally, I believe the pros outweigh the cons, but I will present both.

The Pros

- A "For Sale" sign alerts everyone passing by that the property is available for sale. This is a fantastic way for a real estate agent to obtain information about who is looking for property in the area and help them get additional business from buyers or users of commercial property. A sign will also publicize an agent's name in an area in which they work.

- Other commercial agents in the area will see the sign, and it will help promote interest from cooperating brokers.

- That rare drive-by user looking for property in the area might just purchase your property.

The Cons

- It announces to the world that the building may be vacant and makes it a target for break-ins or possible vandalism.

Question: I want to reduce the commission. What are the pros and cons?

Answer: There are certainly strong pros and strong cons to reducing a real estate commission. Obviously, if you are the owner of a commercial real estate property and are about to sell it, you want to reduce your expenses as much as possible; this may include the commission.

Real estate commissions are generally 6% of the sales price. Let's say you are thinking of reducing them to 5%. Understand you are not just reducing your outgoing expense but reducing your agent's motivation and any cooperating broker's motivation.

The one thing I have noticed after many years in the business is that what drives real estate agents more than anything is motivation: motivation in the form of money. When the commission is reduced from the outset, so is the motivation.

A real estate agent who isn't as motivated because of a reduced commission might put in less effort, which means your property could take more time to sell.

Pulling the curtain back a bit more . . .

Remember, your building may not be the only building available for sale. When cooperating brokers realize they are only receiving 2.5% (half of 5%) on a building instead of 3%, they are more likely to show and promote a higher-commission building than a lower-commission building. They shouldn't do this, but it's human nature. The more you can keep your broker's commission close to the industry standard, the more motivated they will be to sell your property.

Once the deal has been negotiated and is almost completed, something always seems to crop up, and the cost is just enough for the seller to look at the broker and their commission as a source to pull funds from. When the real estate broker has a 6% commission to work with, they may be more willing to "chip in" than if the starting point was only 5%. If you, as an owner, have to bridge a gap at the eleventh hour to complete the transaction, you have more leverage with a broker to reduce the commission at that time than any other.

Maximum Exposure for Marketing a Building

Question: How will I be sure the agent is giving my property the maximum exposure?

Answer: There are many different ways to market a property, and if your broker has explained them all, then you can check to see if each one of these items is being completed. Has a sign been installed in a timely fashion? Has the listing been published on multiple listing services? Has the broker sent out a mailing and published a brochure and a floor plan? Has the broker cold-called the neighborhood? There are many items that you, as the owner of a property, can easily check and monitor throughout the listing period. In the end, it all boils down to communication between you and your broker.

Question: I have heard that once an agent gets a listing, they sit on it for a while. Is this true? If so, what can be done about it?

Answer: Yes. In my thirty-plus years as a broker, I have seen other agents obtain a listing and sit on it for a number of days or even weeks while they try to find a buyer on their own so they can receive the entire commission and not have to split it with an outside broker. I would say the majority of brokers only do this for two or three business days before publishing the listing and making fellow agents aware of it.

On the flip side, I also know brokers who will advertise a listing to other brokers before they even obtain the listing so they can act quickly for the owner of the property.

If your broker alerts you to important milestones, such as the publication of brochures, installation of signs, and appearance on multiple listing services, you can be confident your property is receiving the maximum exposure to the maximum number of people.

Before you sign the listing agreement, you have leverage to make some reasonable demands. Some of those demands could include setting a timeline to add the property to various multiple listing services and a specific date for the completion of a brochure, floor plans, and other important marketing materials.

You should also schedule a meeting one week after listing with an agent to check on the progress of all the various marketing activities.

Question: I want to know what is going on with the listing of my property and don't want to be left in the dark. How do I go about this?

Answer: Throughout the marketing process, you should be informed on a regular basis as to the status of the marketing effort and the response to that effort.

You should never have to call the listing agent to find out what is happening. On the contrary, you should be informed as major events occur (i.e., advance notices, brochures, mailings, showings of the property, and, of course, all offers to purchase the facility).

You should make it clear to the broker from the outset that communication is imperative and you don't want to be left in the dark. You should demand or at least encourage a regular marketing meeting or conference call to discuss what action *has* occurred and *will* occur, as well as a general conversation regarding how to adjust the marketing strategy to the ever-changing competition or market conditions.

IMPROVEMENTS

Question: Can I sell my building "as is"?

Answer: The quick answer is, yes. However, there are certain minimum conditions that must be fulfilled.

I have worked with many sellers who say they do not want to put a penny into a property they are selling, even if they know they would receive a higher sales price if they did. But many buyers ask sellers for particular improvements, modifications, or adjustments to the property, which means the property isn't being sold "as is." Depending on which state or city the property is located in, a government agency may also have to document the existence or absence of one or more particular items the seller must complete before the sale.

Quick Thought: Try to stay away from advertising the building as being in "as is" condition. Most buyers will then expect a property in rough or rundown condition and consequently have a much more critical eye in searching for anything that might be wrong with the building, and this could contribute to undercutting your sales price.

True Story

Question: How can trash removal, a coat of paint, and a few flowers earn you $161,000?

Answer: I was given a listing on a building that was in dire need of some enhancement, and the owner decided to take my advice and obtain some bids on cleanup, including repairing the asphalt, painting the exterior of the building, and landscaping. The final estimate the owner received totaled $41,300. I contacted contractors I knew and received bids on the same work totaling only $9,465, a savings of over $31,000.

These enhancements were completed, and they increased the value of the building by $8 to $10 per square foot, or a minimum of $161,000. The seller received a record price on the sale—certainly much more than she anticipated. This is another overlooked area in which the right real estate agent can save you money.

Question: Will flowers, trees, and grass help me get a higher sales price?

Answer: Many times, yes! A little bit of yard work can add true curb appeal to a commercial building.

Trimming a tree next to a building can make the building look larger and newer! Planting some flowers or plants can make a building's entrance look more inviting and give the impression the seller cares about the property. Keeping the property clean and tidy by pulling up weeds and picking up trash in the parking lot has an incredible effect too.

I once received a listing on an industrial building that had trees and bushes all along the street frontage. It was difficult to see the building from the street. I convinced the owner to hire a tree trimmer to thin out the trees and bushes. Once completed, I started receiving calls from the neighbors simply to comment on how nice the building finally looked from the street. I also referred the tree trimmer to a neighbor who wanted his property cleaned up. And yes, I received multiple offers and sold the building for, at the time, the highest price per square foot for a building in the area.

©Marty Bucella   www.martybucella.com

"Today I laughed all the way to the bank, but I was crying on the inside. Just kidding. I was laughing on the inside, too."

Question: This is a dirty industrial building. Why should I clean up the property before selling?

Answer: Doing some housekeeping inside and outside the building and cleaning up any untidiness can help enhance the look and usability of the property for sale.

If you were a buyer walking into a dirty, messy building, would you also suspect that the things you *couldn't* see might be messy, dirty, or not maintained? For instance, the sprinkler system, roof maintenance, HVAC system, etc.

If you, as a seller, clean up the obvious messes and show that the building is maintained, it will help eliminate many issues that a buyer might otherwise consider investigating more thoroughly.

Remember this: if the obvious things need maintenance, then how much work do the inconspicuous items need?

Quick Thought: During the time your property is on the market, maintain the electrical service to the property. The building and property will show better when the lights can be turned on.

Question: What is a parking ratio, and why is it important for my building?

Answer: The parking ratio is the amount of automobile parking that can be accomplished on your parcel compared to the total size of your building.

For example, a common parking ratio for industrial buildings is 2 to 1. This just means there are two marked parking spaces for every thousand square feet of building area. So, an 8,000-square-foot building with a 2-to-1 parking ratio would have sixteen marked parking spaces.

In higher-parked facilities, such as research and development facilities where there might be additional office space inside the building (more workers equal more parking spaces needed), the parking ratio might be 3 to 1. So, an 8,000-square-foot building with a 3-to-1 parking ratio would have twenty-four marked parking stalls. (Your fourth-grade math is paying off!)

Parking ratios can be 1 to 1, as with warehouse-only buildings; 4 to 1, as with many office buildings; 5 to 1, as with many auto-use facilities; and all the way up to 10 to 1 or higher for other special-use facilities.

The term "overparked" means that an industrial building that would normally have a 2-to-1 parking ratio might have a 2.5-to-1 or 3-to-1 parking ratio. Being "overparked" can be beneficial when marketing a commercial building because you can highlight how the higher parking ratio could be used:

- to accommodate additional office space within the building

- to create "secured parking" by enclosing part of the parking area within a fence

- to store materials outside within a fenced yard

STRATEGY

Question: How do I price my building?

Answer: Have you heard of the saying, "I know just enough to be dangerous"? Well, don't be dangerous to yourself! Maybe you saw a building that was the same size as yours, and it recently sold. So, you price your building close to the same amount. Later, you discover that the building you based your price on had an expensive foundation problem. Now, your building is being sold for well below what it should be. Yes, that is definitely dangerous!

This demonstrates why you need the help and experience of a commercial real estate broker—someone who has experience in the area in which your building is located and knows why a building sold . . . and why it sold for a particular price. It's one thing to review a list of sold buildings; it's quite another to try to determine which ones compare to your property.

To price your building to attain the highest sales price possible, you need to know the many facets of the market. It is very difficult to do that unless you personally work in that market on a day-to-day basis. What amenities does your building have compared to other buildings that have sold or are up for sale? Does the zoning lend itself to obtaining a higher sales price, etc.? To achieve the best possible price for your property, the services of a commercial real estate broker are imperative.

Question: How long will it take to sell my building?

Answer: How long it takes to sell your building depends on many factors. Of course, the most important factor is the price. If the price is much higher than the market, it will probably stay on the market longer and be one of the last to sell until either the market catches up with the price or the seller reduces the price.

Properties on the market for too long can become stagnant and harder to sell because even if the price is reduced, it may take some time for the property to be reintroduced and gain favor in the marketplace. If your building is priced at the high end of the market, just make sure there is a reason for it: location, special amenities and improvements, special zoning, etc.

If the price is too low, you might receive many offers, and the building may be on the market for a shorter period of time. But you don't want to price it so low that you have a pile of purchase offers. You have to strike a balance.

Once an offer has been received, negotiations can last anywhere from a few hours to a few days depending on the intricacies of the price terms, amenities, the principals involved, and other items of importance.

Contingencies such as environmental studies, title issues, and financing can prolong an escrow. Because a contingency in a purchase agreement expires after a period of time (e.g., thirty days), the buyer may ask the seller for an extension of the contingency period. The buyer and seller may have to work on it for a while depending on the complexity of the situation and the cooperation of the principals.

I have been involved in escrows that have taken only three business days from beginning to end, and I have been involved in escrows that lasted longer than one year. Usually, however, once a property has entered escrow, the time to close the escrow is anywhere from sixty to ninety days.

Calculating from the moment a property first becomes available for sale, a general timeline might be as follows: four weeks to market the property, one to two weeks to receive offers, one to two weeks to negotiate the offers, and one and a half to three months to close the escrow. So, from start to finish, it could take anywhere from four to five months. Always be prepared for the process to take longer.

Question: How can I get my listing agent totally committed to me and the ultimate success of selling my building?

Answer: One important thing you can do is have the listing agent agree not to work on any listings in the immediate area that are perceived as direct competition.

Get a list of all the current listings that the agent has and determine if any of them are competing with your property. Also, this is a good chance to see just how many listings the agent has available. Will they be able to spend an adequate amount of time on your property? If the agent has ten listings, do they work on two listings a day? By that standard, the agent will get to your property once a week—maybe not the amount of attention you want. It is counterproductive to have too many listings or listings that compete against one another.

<u>Another possible conflict of interest to be aware of:</u>

If an interested buyer does not purchase your building but still wants to search for a property to purchase, this will pull your listing agent's focus away from selling your building. Instead, their focus will be on showing other properties to a buyer who is not interested in your building.

If this happens (and many times, it will), have an agreement with your listing agent to refer those buyers to *another* agent so your agent's focus can remain on selling your property and representing *your* best interests.

Question: My building is leased for another four years. Can I sell it now?

Answer: Yes, you can market and sell your property with your tenant in place. In this case, the buyer would actually be purchasing the lease income that the property generates over the next four years. Bear in mind, those buyers are investors, and investors will pay what the income stream generates, not necessarily what the real property is worth on the open market to a user.

Here is a rough (very rough) example to illustrate my point. Your 5,000-square-foot building has an income of $4,000 per month ($48,000 per year). $48,000/5.5% = $873,000. An investor who wants a 5.5% return on their investment will pay $873,000, or about $174 per square foot. To a user of the property, the building may be worth $1 million, or about $200 per square foot.

I have also seen buildings sell to an investor for a very low return on investment. This is due in large part to the particular tenant occupying the building. Some of these investments with well-known tenants such as Starbucks, etc., have sold for as low as a 1% return, making the income on the lease worth much more than the actual real estate. A major problem occurs when the well-known tenant moves out and you have to lease the property to a lesser-known tenant for a much lower price. Watch out because the property's value can plummet.

Question: I own a building with a partner. I want to sell, but my partner does not. What can I do?

Answer: Before purchasing real estate with a partner or a partnership group, it is important to have an exit strategy. Never go into any investment without first knowing how you would sell it. You may think you want to hold onto the property forever, but you never know when you might want to or have to sell the property in the future.

To be able to sell your portion of the real estate while allowing your partner or partners to retain their ownership interests, the ownership should be held as tenants in common. This way of holding title allows you to sell your portion to anyone, while the other partners retain their ownership.

Regarding partnership agreements, there should be language in the agreement stating exactly how a partner can sell their interest. Partners of a property often have a first right of refusal to purchase any of the other partners' interests in the property. In reality, all partners should have a first right of refusal clause in any partnership agreement. As a seller, your interest in the property is worth more to an existing partner than to an outsider, which in most cases will result in a higher selling price for you.

When purchasing any investment property, it's a good idea to invest in a few hours with a highly regarded real estate attorney to prepare the proper documentation for partnership agreements, LLCs, or any other type of real estate partnership agreement.

Question: Will certain buyers pay more for a particular building than other buildings?

Answer: If a building has an inordinate amount of electrical power, it stands to reason that the most likely tenant for that building will be a manufacturing company or a company that uses a lot of electrical power. A warehouse and distribution tenant only needs enough electricity to turn the lights on. Buildings with a large amount of electrical power might be worth more to a manufacturing company than to a warehouse and distribution company. On the other hand, a building with dock-high loading doors would be worth more to a warehouse and distribution company than a manufacturing company. Buyers will pay a premium for a building if it has particular improvements that the buyer needs to help operate their business.

Certain types of zoning can make a building worth much more to a particular type of business too. Examples include auto zoning or zoning that permits the sale of marijuana. A building that can accommodate auto uses can sometimes be worth anywhere from 20% to 100% more than if the property did not have that zoning. As for zonings that permit marijuana sales, rates can be, as the Beatles profess in "Lucy in the Sky with Diamonds," "incredibly high." Younger readers: go buy this album.

Question: I put my building up for sale, and I received four offers in two days. Is that a good thing? Or did I price it too low?

Answer: Hey, you wanted to sell, and now you're complaining? Actually, the quick answer is, yes, it is priced too low. But when we peel back the layers to uncover why multiple offers have been received, we discover that there could be some very good reasons.

Some markets have a very low vacancy rate, so you may receive multiple offers, even if a property is priced appropriately. This could be because many buyers or users are waiting on the sidelines for a specific type of property to become available. Once it does, they are all alerted at the same time and boom: multiple offers.

If your facility is priced too low, you will get a greater response from buyers, which could also result in more than one offer at a time. When you do receive multiple offers, if you determine that your property is priced too low, there's no steadfast rule that you must agree to the published price. If you wish, you can respond to the offer with a *higher* sales price.

Hopefully, you have chosen your real estate broker well. So, if you do receive multiple offers, it's because there are many people waiting on the sidelines for your specific type of facility. In that case, a bidding war could ensue.

Question: What do I do if I get two or three offers at the same time?

Answer: Any time multiple offers are received on a property, my first thought might be that the property is listed too low. More than likely, though, there's a pent-up demand for that type of property in that particular area that attracts buyers and culminates in multiple offers to purchase.

There are different schools of thought on how to respond when you receive multiple offers. Some sellers will respond to the most financially fit buyer and not respond to any others. In other words, they will respond to one buyer at a time. Other sellers might respond to all offers at the same time to see which buyer(s) will respond—and how they will respond. Only a mutually signed purchase agreement can bind the parties, so this option is the optimal way to determine who is the best buyer for the property. Plus, you may incite a bidding war, which will increase the sales price of your property.

Question: What if I get a lowball offer?

Answer: Some sellers and brokers feel that lowball offers shouldn't even merit a response.

However, I have seen many lowball buyers end up paying the listed price for a property they previously submitted a low offer on. Buyers like to see if they can get a deal or obtain the best possible price, and some do this by submitting offers far below the asking price.

You should respond to all offers so all buyers are aware that you have recognized them as a possible buyer and given them a realistic price at which you would sell the property. Even if the response restates the asking price, you should respond to all written offers with a written response.

Question: What if I do not receive any offers on my building?

Answer: If it is approaching thirty to forty-five days and you have not received an offer, step back and examine the sales activity on your property. Has the listing been advertised in the multiple listing services? Have a brochure and floor plan been published and distributed? Is there a "For Sale" sign on the property? Have mailings gone out? Have prospective buyers toured the property?

If you answered "yes" to all of these questions, then why have you not received an offer? If there were tours, what happened to the prospective buyers who toured the property? What other comparable properties have sold in the area, if any? Once you have answered these additional questions, you will have a better idea of why you have not received an offer.

Could it be the asking price? Is the building functionally obsolescent? You may have to take a hard look at whether the pricing is correct, the marketing is correct, and your real estate agent is correct. Never be afraid to ask the tough questions, get the real answers, and make adjustments.

Question: I'm selling my multi-tenant building, and the buyer is requesting an estoppel certificate. What is that?

Answer: An estoppel certificate is a signed statement by a party (usually the tenant) certifying for another's benefit (usually the owner) that the lease actually exists. It also certifies the amount of the monthly rent, that there are no defaults under the lease, and that the rent is paid up to a certain date.

Buyers of property with existing tenants usually want to ascertain and have some assurance that the tenants in the building are paying what the owner of the property says they are paying. The owner can show the buyer a lease, but the buyer must have confirmation from the actual tenant. The estoppel certificate is confirmation by the tenant that these are, indeed, the facts of the current lease.

Sometimes for banking or accounting reasons, the lender on a property may ask the tenants to complete an estoppel certificate to confirm the rental amount the owner has declared is true. There is no case in which a buyer purchasing an investment property with existing tenants should forgo requesting an estoppel certificate.

Question: Is there a good time of year to sell a property?

Answer: Some periods of the calendar year can be better than others.

For residential property, the school of thought is to put a house on the market in the springtime because many people are in the mood to look for homes, and families with children can purchase a house and move in before the next school year.

However, as an owner of commercial property, you may be restricted by conditions that dictate when to put your property on the market. It could be when the lease expires or when you retire, if you occupy the building. Many different conditions can influence when you might bring a building to the market for sale.

Nevertheless, it is worth noting that there is typically a slowdown in the marketplace during the summer months, with activity picking back up in late summer to early fall. The majority of leases expire in September, October, and November, probably because when the summer ends, people tend to go back to work and realize that a new facility is necessary. More leases are entered into at this time of the year, and since all leases expire, they expire at this time of the year as well. If you have the luxury to choose, the months of September and October would be favorable for listing a property and bringing it to the marketplace.

Question: If I'm selling my property, do I need to get an appraisal?

Answer: If you are going to sell your commercial property, an appraisal is like chicken soup: it can't hurt. But the price of an appraisal might.

I can never understand why residential appraisals cost $500, but a commercial property appraisal might cost anywhere from $2,500 to $10,000. Appraisers receive much of their information from commercial real estate brokers, so ultimately, if you are involved with a commercial real estate broker, you should be able to get a pretty good evaluation without spending thousands of dollars for the information. See, you are already saving money, and you just started!

If your commercial real estate broker is active in your area, it should be a quick process to get you an accurate evaluation of what your property might actually sell for. This is something most commercial real estate brokers should supply a seller.

Question: Is zoning important when selling a building?

Answer: Zoning is extremely important in commercial real estate. If a property is zoned for warehouse and distribution and a company wants to move in and do retail sales, it would not be able to operate legally, unless you applied for and obtained a conditional use permit (CUP).

If you are looking to sell a property that is zoned for auto use, you might have a smaller population of businesses to market to, but those businesses might have a greater demand for your property because fewer auto-zoned properties exist. So, your auto-zoned property may be worth more.

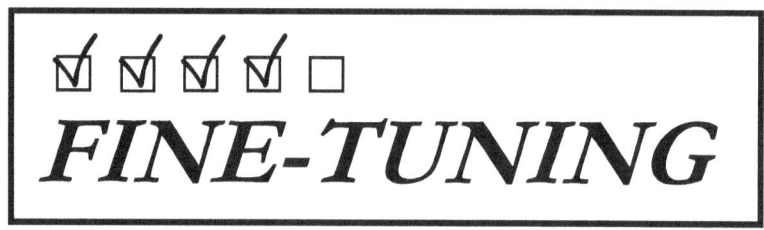

FINE-TUNING

Question: Hazardous substances? What does that mean? What is a Phase 1, and what is a Phase 2? Is there such a thing as a Phase 3?

Answer: You might hear the terms "hazardous substances," "environmental studies," or "Phase 1 studies." They all refer to the same thing.

When purchasing a commercial property, you want to be assured you are buying a clean site absent of any contamination in the soil from previous users or other sources. In some instances, the cleanup of a contaminated site can far outweigh the entire value of the property. Therefore, you want to protect yourself to make sure you are not inheriting a contaminated site. In almost all cases, the lending institution that holds the mortgage for a commercial property, especially industrial property, will require an environmental study to provide proof that the site is clean and free of hazardous substances or contamination. After all, the lending institution does not want to get involved with a dirty, hazardous site.

"The good news is, you won't need any night time security lighting."

Question: What are hazardous substances and contamination?

Answer: Anything not normally found in the soil that could pose a potential environmental problem. Examples: crude oil, grease, paint, transmission oil, chemicals, solvents, acid, glue, pesticides, and heavy metals, to name a few.

In order to determine whether a site is clean and free of contamination, an environmental study known as a Phase 1 study is conducted. A Phase 1 study involves an environmental testing company physically walking around and inspecting the property to look for any signs that could lead them to conclude that there might be contamination, such as an oil pit, grease or chemical stains in the building or parking lot, an area of dead vegetation, or improperly stored fifty-five-gallon drums full of chemicals, to name a few.

Government files, such as the records of the local fire department, will also be searched to determine whether any chemical spills have occurred, as well as any event that might have required a response from the fire department or site cleanup by a hazardous substance team. Prior uses and occupants of the building are also researched to determine whether the types of businesses that were previously in the building might have contaminated the property in any way. Businesses that cannot escape the eye of a Phase 1 researcher are dry cleaners, auto uses, and metal platers.

After the exhaustive study, if everything comes back clean or acceptable to the researcher, the report will conclude there is no further action needed, and the site is deemed environmentally clean. If, however, there is some suspicion that there could be hazardous substances in or around the building, the Phase 1 report might recommend that a Phase 2 study be conducted in order to determine the cleanliness of the site.

A Phase 2 study entails taking actual samples of soil from the site and testing them in a laboratory to determine if any hazardous substances are present in the soil. The samples are taken by drilling and removing a core sample of soil. They can be taken at various depths and in various locations in and around the property.

If the soil samples come back clean, all is well. The soil test can even come back a little contaminated as long as it is below the threshold of what is deemed safe by whichever government agency has jurisdiction in that area. However, if it comes back in excess of those thresholds, a more expansive Phase 2 study might be recommended to better define the size and extent of the contamination. Once an area of contamination is defined, an environmental company may recommend ways to remove it or reduce it by conducting a Phase 3.

In the case of actual soil contamination, a Phase 3 involves removing the contaminated soil, checking the site adjacent to the contaminated soil to make sure it is clean, then refilling and repacking the area with clean soil. This can be quite expensive. Sometimes a Phase 3 can include the removal of trapped gases, and it can take quite some time to reduce those gases to an acceptable level. It might involve collecting gases from the soil and continuing to collect them until the level of contaminated gas is below an acceptable threshold. One piece of good news is that a Phase 3 is rare.

True Story

They say you never forget your first building sale. Mine was one that would be hard to forget under any circumstances.

One early morning, I received a call from a lady with a very thick Eastern European accent. It was very hard to understand her, but I fought through it the best I could. She wanted to purchase an industrial building in Orange County as soon as possible. She was moving her chemical business out of the Los Angeles area and wanted to move into a new location right away.

I advised her that it would be much faster to occupy a building if she were to lease one, but she insisted that she wanted to own the building. So, I told her I would put together a survey of available buildings and could show her what was available the next day. She said that would be fine, but I would have to come pick her up, as her car was not working. When I asked for her address, she gave me an address in Studio City, an area north of Los Angeles County that was almost sixty miles away from where I did business in Orange County.

I was so full of enthusiasm that I didn't care where she was located. So, I drove all the way to Studio City, picked her up, and drove all the way back to Orange County to tour three or four industrial buildings. After our tour, I drove her back to Studio City, dropped her off, then turned around and drove back home to Orange County. She decided on one of the buildings I had shown her pretty quickly. We made an offer on it, the offer was accepted, and we entered escrow.

That same night, I was watching the local news, and a story came on about a chemical plant in North Los Angeles County that had caught fire, burned down, and left a chemical hazard in its wake. The authorities were looking for the owner of the chemical business and actually had a video of the owner on the surveillance camera of the next-door business. I got a sick feeling in my stomach. The story and the timing of this was very coincidental, and it sounded all too familiar to me.

As I watched the blurry surveillance video, I could still recognize the person in the video as my Studio City Buyer. The next morning, I called her and asked her about the story on the news. Her response was cryptic. She and her attorney were taking care of things, she said, and all would be worked out soon. To make a very intriguing, long story short, things were worked out, escrow closed, and she moved into the building for the next few years but never operated a chemical business there.

Question: Who pays for the Phase 1, Phase 2, and Phase 3 studies?

Answer: In almost all cases, the Phase 1 study is paid for by the buyer. The Phase 2 is usually paid for by the buyer too, but sometimes the cost is shared with the seller, especially if the seller is anxious or motivated to sell the property.

After a Phase 2 study is conducted, a buyer will determine whether or not it is financially worth it to continue pursuing the contaminated property or if they would be better off finding another property. In the Phase 3 studies that I have been involved with, the buyer has paid for such remediation in every case.

Environmental studies are important and should never be overlooked.

Question: How do I know I'm getting top dollar for the sale of my building?

Answer: The real estate broker you chose to sell your property should have given you the market value of your property based on what comparable properties in the area have sold for, plus their current asking prices. You should have a general idea of what your building should sell for before it is placed on the market.

If you like, you can obtain a professional appraisal of the property. However, many appraisals will be conservative, somewhat undercutting what the current market rate might be. Ultimately, you want to obtain the highest price possible, and maybe the sale of your building will end up setting a new high-water mark in your particular market that would not necessarily show on an appraisal.

As I mentioned earlier, the appraisers get their information from commercial real estate brokers in the area. So, if you hire a good commercial real estate broker, this information should be available to you without having to pay for the cost of an appraisal.

By comparing previously sold buildings and studying the direction of the market, you and your broker will have a good indication as to what constitutes "top dollar."

Question: I want to reduce the contingency period. Can we eliminate contingencies?

Answer: As a seller, that is sometimes difficult to do. All buyers need a certain amount of time to inspect a property, make sure it is environmentally sound, and confirm there is a good title, among other things. There are specified time periods during escrow in which to complete all the contingencies, and it is sometimes hard to hurry that process.

I have been involved in a few sales where the seller demanded the buyer complete all of the contingencies prior to escrow *opening*. This is when the buyer spends time and money to investigate all aspects of the property. However, this is a very rare occurrence, and I would not recommend that a buyer complete their contingencies prior to the opening of escrow.

Question: What if a buyer cannot get a loan to purchase my building? Is this a waste of time?

Answer: Yes, it is a waste of time. However, to mitigate these circumstances, it's always best to obtain a letter of prequalification from the buyer's lending institution stating that the buyer qualifies for the amount of the loan necessary to purchase the property. This way, you lower the chances of a buyer not closing an escrow simply because they can't obtain a loan.

It might be helpful to obtain some financial documentation on the buyer and get to know the buyer's history of operating a business.

Question: If I receive multiple offers on my building, which one do I choose?

Answer: That is a great problem to have. Ultimately, the goal is to sell your property for the highest price; therefore, the price offered by the buyer is important. However, the likelihood of the buyer obtaining the financing for the purchase is just as important. Look at the financial strength of the buyer, look at their motivation, and look for a prequalification letter from a lending institution as well.

You might try to find out if the buyer is financially able to make up the difference in the down payment if the appraisal turns out to be less than the agreed-upon purchase price (since the bank might decrease the amount of the loan).

An additional step you might want to take is to meet each of the possible buyers at their present place of business to get a good overall feel for their motivation. This may be a good way to see how sincere each buyer is about closing the deal and how likely it is that the deal will actually close.

Question: Who picks the escrow company, the title company, and the inspection companies?

Answer: As the seller, you have the upper hand and the leverage to choose whatever escrow company you like. If you have no preference, sometimes the buyer might prefer a particular escrow company. In reality, there is not much difference between escrow companies. As long as it is a company you have heard of or one that has been in business for a while, it should be all right. Just be sure the escrow company routinely handles commercial property.

As for a title company, since you, the seller, must pay for title insurance, you can choose which title company to use. You might ask who your real estate agent uses, as real estate agents often have relationships with title companies and title officers that can make the title process much easier, especially if a situation arises with the title. Some agents may also receive a discount on title work that you can benefit from.

When it comes to inspections of the property, the buyer usually pays for all inspections and, therefore, can choose any inspection company they desire.

CLOSING

Question: How long will escrow be?

Answer: That depends. If the buyer has all of the cash and can eliminate the financing contingency portion, which can be the most time-consuming of all the contingencies, then the escrow period can be shortened. A buyer's financing contingency can be as short as thirty to forty days or as long as 120 days depending on the type of loan the buyer is pursuing.

Sometimes an escrow can be extended because of environmental studies, reports, and further investigations if there is any question as to the cleanliness of the property's soil. I don't know of many escrows that have been less than thirty days, even in cases where there was no financing contingency and the buyer had a briefcase full of cash. The list of contingencies that *any* buyer will insist on still takes some time.

Look for an escrow to take anywhere from forty-five to ninety days, but as a seller, always try to close an escrow as quickly as possible. Too many unforeseen events can crop up during the escrow period that will either extend the escrow or derail it completely.

True Story

One afternoon, I received a call from a man who said he wanted to sell a very small property in Anaheim, about a half mile from Disneyland. The property had been used as a truck scale and had one small six-foot by five-foot shack and a cement pad that was the actual truck scale. The seller had even identified a ready and willing buyer but did not know how to complete the transaction. I said I would be more than happy to help him sell the property, but it seemed as if he had done a lot of the work already.

I met him and told him I would get things organized, complete the paperwork, and contact the title company and escrow company for him. He said that was taken care of. I felt almost useless but went along with everything to see what assistance I could provide. The buyer and seller agreed to a three-day escrow, and everything was completed on time to everyone's satisfaction. The total value of the transaction was $14,000—the smallest sales transaction of my career.

Once the escrow closed, I tried to come up with a way to purchase the property from the new owner and use it to install an advertising billboard, but the city would not allow it. The new owner opened up a locksmith business that also made copies of keys. The last I saw, it was vacant. Any takers?

Question: Does it matter which escrow company or title insurance company I use?

Answer: If you don't use escrow companies and title companies as often as a commercial real estate agent does, it's important to do some shopping and gain some knowledge. You can have your commercial real estate agent tell you exactly how much each escrow company and title insurance company will charge and the benefits of each of those particular companies.

First, investigate which escrow companies are active in the commercial real estate market in your area. That way, the escrow company doesn't have to reinvent the wheel because they will already know how to properly handle a commercial real estate transaction. You might also want to compare escrow companies' fees and see if there is a drastic difference in what they charge for what they actually do.

The same strategy can be applied to title companies. Once again, a little bit of investigation can go a long way. Find out which title companies are the strongest and have the most experience in commercial real estate in your area. The price for title insurance will probably be about the same from one title company to another, so determine which company will give you the best service. Your commercial real estate broker might also have some recommendations.

Question: What are my costs when I sell? Can I reduce them?

Answer: As a seller, the costs consist mostly of the escrow fee, the cost for title, and the real estate brokerage commission.

The escrow fee is generally based on the total purchase price of the property, as is the cost of title insurance, and, of course, the commission is based on the total cost of the building. This is before the cost of any rehab, remodel, or necessary repair work to help the property look its best. As for reducing any of these costs, look to your real estate broker, as they may have relationships with escrow companies, title insurance companies, and contractors if any improvements to the property are warranted. See the next question and answer for more info.

Question: My property is in escrow. What do I do while I'm waiting for the buyer's contingencies to pass?

Answer: The one thing you should not do is sit on your hands. Even though the majority of the contingency investigations are on the buyer's side, there are some contingencies the seller must complete as well.

These will vary, but generally, the seller must complete a seller's mandatory disclosure statement. This is a form that discloses to the buyer whether the property is in a natural hazard zone, such as an earthquake zone, a fire hazard zone, or a flood zone. It also discloses other issues, such as whether the water heater has been braced.

Another item that you, the seller, must provide to the buyer is a property information sheet. This will disclose whether the seller knows of any of the following: material physical defects to the building, issues with the equipment within the building, issues with the soil conditions, the presence of hazardous substances or mold, existing government proceedings or actions on the property, existing or pending lawsuits or proceedings against the seller or the property, etc. The seller must also provide the buyer with copies of any other agreements or items they know of that will affect the property after closing.

It's a good idea to ask the escrow company and the buyer if there are any other documents or if there is any other information they feel might be necessary that you are able to provide.

Question: What if there is a title problem? Can this complicate or extend the escrow?

Answer: Any title problems or situations that cloud the title in any way can create a question of clear title and need to be removed from the exceptions to title prior to the escrow closing.

Some title situations, such as an abandoned easement, can be removed rather easily. But other title situations can be more complex and may have complicated solutions to resolve an exception that interferes with clear title on the property. This could take anywhere from a few days to many days depending on the complexity of the situation or type of lien.

I would recommend that you obtain the preliminary title report on the property you want to sell prior to putting it on the market. This will give you a firsthand look at the liens or claims others have placed on your property, and you can act on them accordingly.

Quick Thought: Obtain a preliminary title report on the property you want to sell (your agent can help you with this). Read it thoroughly and confirm there is no claim to title or lien that may take time to clear up and possibly delay or cancel an escrow.

Question: I am in escrow with the buyer, and the buyer's contingency period has expired. Now, the buyer wants to extend the contingency period, making the escrow take longer. What do I do?

Answer: As a seller, you have already made the mental decision to sell your property, so once you are in escrow, you are ready for the escrow to close as soon as possible. The last thing you want is to have the escrow extended. However, we live in the real world, and escrows must often be extended for certain reasons.

Some reasonable excuses for extending an escrow or the contingency period in an escrow might include the following:

- researching title information
- conducting a Phase 1 that turns into a Phase 2 environmental report
- taking longer than anticipated for appraisals
- completing inspection reports
- financing (the big one)

If the buyer makes a reasonable request to extend a contingency period, as much consideration should be given to the request as possible. After all, you would not want to end an escrow and have to start all over, especially if the request is for an extension of a few days and is reasonable. However, if granting the buyer additional time results in additional costs to the seller, the seller might consider asking the buyer to pay for the extra time.

For example, say the buyer is requesting an additional thirty days for a contingency period. You might grant an additional ten days, and every day after that might be at a cost of $200 a day over and above the purchase price. This might act as a catalyst and push the buyer to work as hard as possible to reduce the amount of time the contingency period is extended.

Question: Can I reduce the escrow fees, title fees, or commission?

Answer: You can shop around at various escrow companies and title insurance companies to see what their customary charge is. The total cost will generally be the same no matter which escrow company or title insurance company is used, but it's always worth talking to a couple of companies to verify their prices. As for commission, the rate can vary as well depending on what you and your real estate agent agree to.

Notwithstanding all of the above, if your agent has a relationship with an escrow company and a title insurance company, as their client, you should receive some of the benefit of that relationship in the form of a reduction in costs. In special circumstances, I have helped pay for some or all of the escrow fees with a portion of the real estate brokerage commission. As a seller, you should always ask for a discount or a reduction in fees.

Question: What if I am in escrow and receive another offer? What do I do?

Answer: Hopefully, in your existing escrow instructions, you or your agent had the foresight to include a paragraph that states that you have the right to accept and negotiate any backup offers at any time during escrow.

You always want to have a Plan B, and negotiating with another buyer, even when your property is in escrow, can be a good insurance policy. Some buyers will not want to negotiate with you when the property is in escrow. They would rather come in and negotiate a deal after an escrow didn't close successfully in order to obtain a better and less expensive result.

A good real estate agent should always keep the names and contact information of all interested parties in order to quickly alert them if a property has fallen out of escrow.

True Story

I once represented a gentleman named Howard who owned a number of commercial properties. He had a small commercial building that had previously been a medical office, and he asked me to list and sell it for him.

One week into marketing the property for sale, I found a buyer to purchase the building. The buyer wanted the seller to carry back a first trust deed of 75% of the purchase price, with the buyer putting 25% of the purchase price as a down payment. Escrow closed, and the new buyer was happy with his purchase and opened up a computer store.

About six months after the escrow closed, the buyer stopped making his mortgage payments to the seller. Although he didn't want to, Howard had no choice but to foreclose on the property and take it back.

Howard asked me to sell the property a second time. In a couple of weeks, I found a new financially fit buyer, and this new buyer also asked Howard to carry a first trust deed and put down 30%. Escrow closed, and in about six or seven months, the buyer ceased making payments, and Howard foreclosed again.

Once Howard obtained the property again, he asked me to list and market the property for yet a third time.

In a couple of weeks, I found a third buyer for Howard. However, this time, the buyer had a bank loan, so Howard did not have the opportunity to carry a first trust deed and was paid all of the cash at the close of escrow.

Howard really wished he would have been able to carry back another first trust deed just in case this buyer also stopped making mortgage payments because it had turned into quite an unexpected moneymaker for him.

Question: I sold a building five years ago. Now, the new owner is contacting me and asking me to pay to fix an item. Do I have to do this?

Answer: A major contingency that the buyer signs off on is an inspection of the building and property. In almost all cases, the buyer will hire a professional inspection company to do the inspection and write up a report identifying those items that are suspect or in need of repair, etc. If there is any question as to the integrity of a portion of the building or any condition the inspector deems in need of repair, the buyer should tell the seller about the items in question and ask the seller to repair or replace the items.

If it was agreed within the purchase agreement for the seller to guarantee specific equipment or portions of the building, then the seller would owe the new owner money for that item. But if, for example, there is a hole in the roof, this would not be the seller's concern. From the moment escrow closes, it is no longer the responsibility of the seller to remunerate the buyer in any way unless there was an item known by the seller to be defective that they did not disclose to the buyer.

"Soup of the day? Mumbo Jumbo Gumbo."

Question: What is a tax-deferred 1031 exchange? Can I do one? Why would I want to do one?

Answer: Okay, that was three questions, and the first one was complex enough. Let's break this down and answer these questions one at a time.

What is a tax-deferred 1031 exchange?

(Also known as "a 1031," "a tax-free exchange," "an exchange," "an up leg," "a Starker exchange," "a three-party exchange," "a simultaneous exchange," "a tax-deferred exchange," "a like-kind exchange," or whatever other fancy name people give it now.)

The term "1031 exchange" is defined under section 1031 of the IRS tax code. 1031 merely refers to the paragraph in the IRS tax code where this lot is found (Section 1031). To put it simply, this strategy allows an investor to "defer" paying capital gains taxes on an investment property when it is sold, as long as another "like-kind property" is purchased with the profit gained by the sale of the first property. This strategy has more benefits than just saving yourself from taxes.

I have heard some people say, "I wasn't able to do a 1031 exchange because I had an industrial building, and I didn't want to exchange into another industrial building." They obviously considered it a "like-kind" type of exchange. While the tax code does refer to like-kind, the new property only needs to be similar to the extent that it's an investment property. It doesn't have to be the exact same type of property that you are exchanging out of.

So, if you have an apartment complex, you don't have to buy another apartment complex; if you have a retail building, you don't have to buy another retail building. You can have an industrial building and exchange it into an apartment complex, or you can have an income-producing parking lot and exchange it into an industrial building. Just as long as there is income derived from the property.

Note: Traditionally, a 1031 exchange is where one property was literally swapped for another like-kind property. However, the likelihood that the property you want is owned by someone who wants your property is really, really slim.

When to Do a 1031 Exchange

When you sell an investment property, even if you weren't the one who initially purchased it, you end up on the hook for capital gains tax.

If you own a rental property that is worth significantly more today than what you (or the original owner) purchased it for, you can make a killing using this powerful strategy. The big question is, how do you actually use this strategy? Continue reading the next section to learn some tips and strategies for success!

How to Do a 1031 Exchange

To use this strategy effectively, you must exchange one property for another property of similar value. In the process, you avoid capital gains, at least for a while.

An investor will eventually cash out and pay taxes, but in the meantime, an investor can trade properties without incurring a sudden tax obligation.

The exchange rules require that both the purchase price and the new loan amount be the same as or higher than the replacement property. This means if an investor was selling a $1 million property that had a $650,000 loan, they would have to buy $1 million or more of replacement property with $650,000 or more in leverage.

Delayed Exchange

The delayed like-kind exchange, which is by far the most common type of exchange chosen by investors today, occurs when the exchanger relinquishes the original property before they acquire a replacement property. In other words, the property the exchanger owns (which is called the "relinquished" property) is transferred first, and the property the exchanger wishes to exchange it for (the "replacement" property) is acquired second.

The exchanger is responsible for marketing their property, securing a buyer, and executing a sale and purchase agreement before the delayed exchange can be initiated. Once this has occurred, the exchanger must hire a third-party exchange intermediary to initiate the sale of the relinquished property and hold the proceeds from the sale in a binding trust for up to 180 days while the seller acquires a like-kind property.

Using this strategy, an investor has a maximum of forty-five days to identify the replacement property and 180 days to complete the sale of their property. In addition to the numerous tax benefits, this extended time frame is one of the reasons the delayed exchange is so popular.

It's important to note that both the original and the replacement property must be within the United States to qualify under section 1031.

Another fun fact: tax deferred exchanges can include more than two properties. For example, you can exchange one property for multiple replacement properties, and vice versa, you can exchange multiple properties for one larger property. As long as the new properties are similar to your original properties, you're good to go. Do yourself a favor and get a good, qualified intermediary to assist you.

Note: There are some additional rules and regulations to a 1031 tax-deferred exchange, but this is not a tax class, nor will we cross that threshold.

Now, if you did not understand any of that, speak to a commercial real estate agent who has completed many 1031 exchanges. Better yet, have a conversation with a tax attorney specializing in 1031 tax-deferred exchanges!

Question: How do I limit or reduce my taxes on the profits from selling my building?

Answer: When you sell a rental property, you have to pay tax on any gain (profit) you earn ("realize," in tax lingo). If you lose money, you'll be able to deduct the loss, subject to important limitations.

Your gain or loss for tax purposes is determined by subtracting your property's adjusted basis on the date of sale from the sales price you receive (plus sales expenses such as real estate commissions).

Your basis in the property (the amount of your total investment in a property for tax purposes) is not fixed. It changes over time to reflect the true value of your investment. This new basis is called the adjusted basis because it reflects adjustments from your starting basis.

Reductions in basis can increase your tax liability when you sell your property because they will increase your gain. Increases in basis will reduce your gain and your tax liability.

Reduction in Basis

Each year, you must subtract the amount of depreciation allowed for the property from the property's basis. This is true regardless of whether you actually claimed any depreciation on your tax return. If you hold on to your property for the full recovery period—27.5 years for residential rental property and 39 years for commercial property—your adjusted basis will be reduced to zero, and there will be nothing left to depreciate.

Your starting basis in the property must also be reduced by any items that represent a return of your cost. These include the following:

- the amount of any insurance or other payment you receive due to a casualty or theft loss

- any deductible casualty loss not covered by insurance

- any amount you receive for granting an easement

Your basis is also reduced if you took the wrong amount of depreciation on your tax return. If you claimed too little depreciation, you must decrease the basis by the amount you should have taken. If you took too much depreciation, you must decrease your basis by the amount you should have deducted plus the part of the excess you deducted that actually lowered your tax liability for any year.

Increases in Basis

You can increase the basis of any property with the following items:

- the cost of any additions or improvements

- amounts spent to restore property after it is damaged or lost due to theft, fire, flood, storm, or another casualty

- the cost of extending utility service lines to the property

- legal fees relating to the property, such as the cost of defending and perfecting the title

Assessments for items that tend to increase the value of your property, such as streets and sidewalks, must be added to the basis also. For example, if your city installs curbing on the street in front of your rental house and assesses you for the cost, you must add the assessment to the basis of your property.

<u>Example</u>

Viola bought a small apartment building and sold it six years later for $300,000. Her starting basis was $200,000. During the time she owned the property, she claimed $43,000 in depreciation deductions and paid $13,000 for a new roof (an improvement). Her depreciation deductions reduced the property's basis, but the roof improvement increased it. Her basis at the time of the sale is $170,000. Viola calculates her taxable gain on the property by subtracting her adjusted basis from the sales price: $300,000 − $170,000 = $130,000.

As you can see, when you sell your property, you effectively give back the depreciation deductions you took on it. Since they reduce your adjusted basis, they increase your taxable gain. So, Viola's taxable gain was increased by the $43,000 in depreciation deductions she took.

The amount of your gain attributed to the depreciation deductions you took in prior years is taxed at a single 25% rate. Viola would have to pay a 25% tax on the $43,000 in depreciation deductions she received. The remaining gain on the sale is taxed at a capital gains rate (usually 15%, but it is 20% for taxpayers in the top tax bracket).

That was an easy example, but if your head exploded, thank goodness there are people (CPAs) who just love this sort of thing. My advice: use them!

Another Example

A train leaves New York City traveling sixty-three miles per hour ... (Just kidding!)

CHAPTER 2 TWO

"Real estate cannot be lost or stolen, nor can it be carried away. Purchased with common sense, paid for in full, and managed with reasonable care, it is about the safest investment in the world."

— Franklin D. Roosevelt

I Am a Buyer Who Wants to Purchase a Property

So, you've been leasing a commercial building for some time now, and you're tired of just paying the rent with little or nothing to show for it. Maybe you're tired of having a landlord and paying for someone else's property. Whatever the reason, you now feel you want to purchase a property and start building your own wealth. By purchasing your own building, you can build equity, stabilize occupancy costs, and preserve cash. Oh, and there *is* the tax thing—income tax deductions that have the potential to save you money every year!

The best advice is, don't rush into it. Gather all the information you think you'll need to determine what and where you want to purchase. Be smart about it. This isn't like buying a pair of pants. This is an important decision, and you should get as much professional advice as possible. Don't buy good when you can buy great!

Some of these questions are from a user's point of view, and some are from an investor's point of view.

Question: I want to buy commercial real estate. What's the first thing I should do?

Answer: Usually, you buy a house when you need to move because you need more living space or want to relocate to a newer, up-and-coming neighborhood. Or perhaps the size of your family has changed. Commercial real estate, however, is much different.

You first need to ask yourself the following questions: Why am I buying commercial real estate? Will this real estate be for investment? Is this property I will use for my business? If it's for my business, why should I purchase when I can lease? Do I plan on selling or exchanging the property in less than ten years?

Once you have answered these questions, the best thing to do is speak to a commercial real estate broker to further explore your motivation for purchasing commercial real estate.

You don't have to hire a broker to go out and start looking for property for you, but at least make an appointment and spend some time with a commercial real estate agent. This will give you a sense of the current marketplace regarding prices and where they might be trending, plus what properties have sold and at what price.

Speaking with a real estate agent will not only inform you about which sales transactions have occurred but will also help you understand why they occurred and give you an accurate view of your local commercial real estate market.

"The big shell is nice, but the property taxes are a killer."

Question: As a pure investor, what type of commercial real estate should I purchase?

Answer: For investors, it boils down to what types of properties make you feel most comfortable. Some people like industrial buildings. Some people like retail strip centers.

On paper, it looks very much the same, but before purchasing commercial real estate, you should try and get a good feel for where you think the market will be in the next five to ten years. Will there still be a need for that retail strip center on Main Street? Will that industrial building on Industrial Way still be needed in ten years?

It's also important to understand the amount of time and effort it takes to rent and manage each type of property. A commercial building of any type, if it has a net lease in place, is one of the least hands-on properties you will own.

An office building might be a challenge after a tenant has moved out and a new tenant wants to move in. Why? Because a tenant improvement list can often include moving walls, ripping up carpet, painting, etc.

On the other hand, some of the easiest buildings to own are industrial buildings. A small industrial building won't run itself, but it almost will. When a tenant vacates the premises, about the only thing you have to do is "hose it out and lease it to another tenant." It's not exactly that easy but awfully close.

It's probably best to contact a commercial real estate agent and discuss how hands-on you would like to be. Have your agent explain the different types of available properties in the area and the pros and cons of each to give you an idea of what you feel most comfortable owning.

Question: As a pure user of commercial property, what type of real estate should I purchase?

In order to deliver the ideal real estate solution, it's important to understand every aspect of your company's operational needs. All aspects of your operations, requirements, and goals should be reviewed to align them with the facility that has the zoning and functionality that suit you. Understanding your requirements is essential in order to be able to compare and distinguish between ideal alternatives.

Important factors to consider are:

- the size of the building (office vs. warehouse)

- the building amenities, such as telecommunications, loading, clearance, electrical power, yard area, and surrounding business support

- the location, such as transportation routes, transportation costs, and shipping logistics

- city zoning ordinances (Where can your business locate?)

- government incentives (Can your business obtain any tax incentives from the city or other government agencies? Can you take advantage of government bond assessments or tax credits from the city or county in which the property is located?)

- the employee pool and commute time

- the various ways to finance the purchase of a facility

- the actual tax rate for this property

The above items are important, but you really need to get out there and walk through a building to get a good understanding of the situation. I have even recommended that buyers who are more than a year away from moving tour a few buildings to get a much broader understanding of the types of facilities that are out there. It's a good way to educate yourself. The more you know, the better off you will be.

Question: Where do I buy commercial real estate?

Answer: That depends. Why do you want to buy commercial real estate? If you want to operate your business from the property you purchase, where your business should be located is more of a business decision. You could select a property that's located in the best area for your employees, close to freeways, near ports of entry, or in a convenient area for your suppliers and customers. However, if you are purchasing a commercial property and intend to be a landlord, then you do not need to be as specific.

The best location to purchase commercial real estate is in an area that you are comfortable with or an area nearby that you are familiar with and can drive to in under an hour.

Investors, if you're up to it, you can purchase commercial real estate outside your area or even in another state. Some buyers will go out of the area or to another state if they can obtain a higher rate of return or a higher lease rate from a tenant.

Here's another observation about industrial property: we've all heard the cliché "location, location, location"; this may not be of importance when it comes to industrial property. Industrial users are the only users I have encountered who do not necessarily care if a building has frontage, as most do not deal with the public or need customers to visit their location. Industrial users usually want to be out of the public eye and don't care about exposure. So, purchasing an industrial building even in a secondary area without much exposure would not have much effect on the lease rate you might charge a tenant, as long as the local vacancy rate is not too high.

Question: How do I buy commercial real estate?

Answer: After speaking with a professional commercial real estate agent, make an appointment and speak to lenders in your area who are actively offering loans for commercial real estate.

Get to know which banks are lending, the interest rates, and the various programs each lender has to offer. Get to know the type of loans that are available to you (conventional, Small Business Administration, etc.) and which loans would be best for your individual situation.

Interview at least two different lenders and compare their loans, rates, programs, and the information and requirements they will need from you. Some lenders are stringent and require reams of paperwork; other lenders do not require as much.

Once you understand the lending process and the different types of loans, it will be much easier for you to understand which direction is best for you and how you can put the purchase of a commercial real estate building together.

If you already have a banking relationship, ask about the types of loans they offer on commercial property. If they don't have a program or a program you like, ask if they can recommend a local lender.

True Story

I was working with a company that was looking to purchase an industrial building to expand their business. We had been working together for several weeks and had reduced the building choices down to only two.

The buyer was okay with either of the two choices but wanted his spiritual adviser to accompany him and give him feedback on the properties during our last tour of each of the buildings. The first building was perfect for the buyer and had all of the amenities he needed, but as we drove into the driveway, both he and the spiritual adviser told me to not even bother shutting off my engine. The building would not work because of the number sequence in the address (really?!). So, I was asked to drive to the next building.

When we arrived at the second and final building, the spiritual adviser walked inside and toured the facility. After completing a thorough walk-through, he walked back out into the front courtyard, pulled out some sort of large ashtray-like bowl, and started a small fire with leaves and vegetation. After waving the smoke about with bird feathers and pacing back and forth in several directions, the spiritual adviser told the buyer that this building would sustain his business, but the business would not thrive.

The buyer decided to put his expansion plans on ice for a while. As time went by, I never saw that company ever expand or purchase any commercial real estate.

Question: My brother/sister/cousin/wife/client/friend is a real estate agent. Maybe I can use them to help me purchase a property, which will save me some money. What do you think?

Answer: I have seen this time and time again. When a buyer has his relative/friend look for commercial real estate, most of the time, that friend is a residential broker.

Here is some dirty little information for you. Many commercial real estate brokers don't have as much respect for residential brokers as some would believe. Many commercial real estate brokers believe residential brokers don't necessarily know the ins and outs of commercial real estate, which sometimes makes them more of a nuisance than an ally in your quest to purchase commercial real estate.

A residential real estate agent doesn't usually have the contacts a commercial agent has cultivated after many years in the field. So, they may not have access to in-depth information.

Residential real estate agents also don't have access to many of the same multiple listing services and additional information that commercial real estate brokers do.

Years ago, I represented a company that put in an offer on a commercial building, and the deal did not come together. I told them about a particular building that might be available for purchase. The company said that they had already made an offer on it, but it was undeliverable or out of their price range. I asked if the building worked for them and if they were still interested in purchasing it. Of course, they said yes. So, I recommended we put in another offer.

We put in a second offer, and after a little negotiation, the parties agreed. A short time later, the property closed escrow. I asked the listing broker why the previous buyer's agent did not close the transaction. The broker explained that the agent was a residential agent who did not understand how a commercial property transaction was put together. The agent incorrectly used a residential purchase offer form, and even after some help from the listing broker, the buyer's agent just gave up.

My recommendation is to use the services of a professional commercial real estate broker and not the services of a family member or friend. You know what they say about doing business with family and friends . . .

Question: What if my offer becomes part of a bidding war?

Answer: Bidding wars on real estate can happen for a number of reasons, one being that there is a lack of supply and an abundance of demand in the marketplace. A bidding war can also occur when a prime and/or popular piece of real estate comes on the market or when interest rates are at such a low level that qualifying for and obtaining loans becomes easier.

So, if you find yourself in a situation where you are not the only interested buyer for a property, expect a bidding war to happen. If it does, be prepared to pay more than you anticipated. When this happens, be careful not to overpay for real estate!

Try to establish an upper limit of the amount you would be willing to pay for a property and compare notes with your real estate broker so you are both in agreement as to what that upper limit is. In rare cases, there may be overriding reasons to continue participating in a bidding war and increasing the amount you are willing to pay.

Here are a few:

- This particular piece of real estate will increase your business more than if your business was located elsewhere.
- The upside value of this property will continue drastically upward because of future development in the area.
- You are privy to information the general public is not yet aware of that this real estate will increase in value markedly.

A rule of thumb if you find yourself in a bidding war: do not pay more than 15% over the asking price. The property will likely be more valuable in the future, and a 15% rise in property value can occur in a reasonable amount of time.

☑ ☑ ☐ ☐ ☐
IMPROVEMENTS

Question: I just completed a walk-through of the building. Do I also need an inspection?

Answer: Yes, you need a professional inspection. I would never recommend purchasing a building without the assistance of a professional building inspector. An inspection of the building by a professional who knows what they are looking for can save you from purchasing something that may cost you many times the cost of an inspection. Be sure that the inspector you hire focuses on inspecting commercial real property.

A professional inspector is familiar with building codes for specific improvements and, in most cases, can tell you whether an improvement to the building is permitted or not. They will crawl into those hard-to-reach spaces and look at the condition of the roof, the foundation, and the floors.

An inspector can also look at electrical distribution, plumbing, HVAC, etc. and determine whether the equipment is in working order and if construction and building codes have been followed.

You don't want to buy yourself a headache. If you are purchasing a building that you know is older and in need of repair, at least know the extent of those repairs and how much they might cost.

Quick Thought: *If you have a business that stacks products, such as a warehouse/distribution business, find out the height limit in the city code to which you are allowed to stack your product under the ceiling beams and fire sprinklers.*

Question: The building I am interested in purchasing has some great offices. I especially like the second-story office space. How do I find out if the office space is permitted and, if so, whether the improvements are built to code?

Answer: It could very well be built to code, but getting capital building improvements permitted and *recognized* as a permitted improvement by the city is another matter.

Even if you do not have a professional building inspector look at the office improvements, you can always go to the city in which the building is located and ask to see the building plans for that particular address. Some cities will give you a roll of plans, but most will give you a thin envelope of microfiche to study. Use this to determine if the improvements to the building are in the city's file and have the proper building permits and licenses. If they do, all is well. If they do not, you might want to see whether you can get the office improvements permitted. A licensed contractor could inspect the improvements and give you a qualified opinion.

If you can't get the improvements permitted, then you certainly don't want to pay for them.

Imagine if the building caught fire or some other catastrophe occurred; you wouldn't want your insurance claim to be rejected because some of the improvements were not permitted. This is a rare case, but it helps to illustrate the importance of knowing if all the building's improvements are permitted.

Question: The building I'm buying already has a conditional use permit (CUP) for the same type of business as mine. This is great! Let's close this escrow!

Answer: Not so fast. Many conditional use permits (CUP) are *conditional*, just like their title states. The CUP was initially granted due to certain requirements that had to be studied and finally approved *conditionally*. A city will approve and let a non-conforming user operate a business if certain conditions set by the city are followed and maintained by the business.

There are many reasons a city might grant a CUP. Maybe the prior occupant needed and obtained a CUP because there wasn't enough parking on site to meet the city's parking code. Maybe a CUP was needed because the actual use wasn't the traditional type of use usually associated with the zone the property was located in. Maybe the hours of operation were outside the accepted working hours as per the existing zoning regulations. Just because a CUP was obtained by the previous occupant doesn't mean that same permit goes with the property. Some CUPs are only valid as long as the original occupant occupies the property, and some CUPs are only valid for a certain period of time.

The best advice is to go to the city's planning desk and specifically ask about the type of CUP the property currently has. Ask why it was obtained and if your business can use the same CUP or if you have to apply for a new one.

You can't fool City Hall and just move in and start your business, at least not in the long run. Sooner or later, a city inspector, the fire department, or a code enforcer will take a look at your facility. So, it's best to do everything by the book, including obtaining a conditional use permit, if needed. You don't want to be fined—or worse, told to cease operations.

Question: The building I'm interested in purchasing has much more parking than I need. Can I convert the extra parking into a fenced yard for storage that will solve my outdoor storage problem?

Answer: This might have been accepted and overlooked years ago, but now almost all city planning departments require that a certain number of parking spaces be free and available for parking cars and not used for storage.

For instance, if you have a 10,000-square-foot industrial building that requires twenty parking places, but you only have three or four employees and only use three or four parking spots, you might be able to fence off the unused parking spaces and tell the city that it is secured parking. Ask the city for a permit to install a fence for this purpose. If the city agrees to your request and allows you to install a fence, the fenced-in area will eventually become a space for outside storage rather than actual secured parking for vehicles. You are taking a chance that the city may revisit the permit it granted and have you clear the parking lot of storage items and return it to a secured parking area. It's a fine line: sometimes it works, and sometimes it doesn't. It just depends on how active the city's code enforcement employees are and how diligent of a job they do.

Quick Thought: Make sure the delivery trucks your company uses can actually be serviced from the loading doors. Verify that they have the staging area needed to make the required turns to safely drive in and load or unload.

Question: The building I have in escrow is 10,000 square feet. It currently has 2,500 square feet of office space. I need 6,000 square feet of office space, which means I have plenty of room to build the additional 3,500 square feet I need, right?

Answer: Maybe, maybe not. It depends on how many parking spaces are currently associated with your building.

If the 10,000-square-foot building has 2 to 1 parking, which means there are twenty parking places in total, the city might look at it this way: 6,000 square feet of office space at four parking places for every 1,000 square feet will require *twenty-four* parking places. Also, 4,000 square feet of warehouse space at two parking places for every 1,000 square feet equals *eight* parking places for a total of *thirty-two* parking spaces. If the property only has *twenty* parking spaces, we need to change our plans, or we need to obtain a conditional use permit (CUP) from the city to build the additional office space despite the lack of parking.

Question: How do I finance my first real estate deal?

Answer: There are a number of options when it comes to financing your first real estate deal. You can always choose a conventional course of action by acquiring a loan from a traditional lender (i.e., big banking institutions), or you can elect to borrow from a private or hard money lender. Private lenders have less strict loan requirements and therefore typically charge higher interest rates.

I suggest you speak to others who have purchased real estate and find out the type of lender they chose and why. Someone who has gone through the process can sometimes be your best source of information. You can also ask a commercial real estate broker about the kinds of transactions they have seen financed. Most commercial real estate agents know a mortgage broker or a banker whom they have worked with in the past, and this can be a great way to obtain more knowledge about financing.

Now that we've touched on loans and financing, let's see what types of financing are available.

Question: What are the different ways to finance the purchase of a building?

Answer: There are a number of different ways to obtain financing for the purchase of a property. Here are some of the more popular options:

- A conventional loan at a bank or lending institution. You typically need a down payment of between 25% and 35% of the purchase price. Conventional loans have interest rates that are lower than many other types of loans but might be somewhat higher than government loan programs.

- <u>A Small Business Administration (SBA) loan from a bank or lending institution.</u> With an SBA loan, you can put down as little as 10% of the purchase price. Interest rates are very competitive and are often the lowest of all other types of loans, including conventional loans.

- <u>A bridge loan.</u> This is a short-term loan that is obtained when you are securing permanent financing somewhere else. A bridge loan is used when you must purchase a property quickly, and you want to secure permanent financing soon after. Interest rates on bridge loans can be higher than on any other loan product.

- <u>A hard money loan.</u> Consider it the loan of last resort. Lenders of hard loans are primarily individuals or companies, not banks. This type of loan is usually taken out for a short period of time as a way to quickly raise money but at a much higher cost. Hard money loans rely on collateral rather than the applicant's financial situation, so the funding time frame is much shorter. Interest rates are generally much higher than market interest rates—sometimes three or four times higher.

"I heard you make loans to small businesses."

Question: What is an SBA loan?

Answer: SBA is one acronym every small business owner needs to know.

The United States Small Business Administration (SBA) offers two types of loan programs: the 504 loan program and the 7(a) loan program. The 504 provides financing for the purchase of fixed assets, which usually means real estate, buildings, and machinery, at or below competitive market rates.

An SBA loan is a small business loan that is partially guaranteed by the government and the SBA, which eliminates some of the risk for the financial institution that is issuing the loan. The SBA is not the lender. They work with a network of approved financial institutions and partially guarantee the loans that these lenders extend to small businesses. This means they will back up part of the loan a small business receives. So, if you are unable to pay back your SBA loan, the lender knows that the SBA will cover the portion that the SBA guarantees. Because SBA loans involve a government entity in their application process, you will need to prepare a lot of documentation and have even more patience, but it can be well worth it.

Just like any other type of loan, SBA loans come in all shapes and sizes. They can range in size up to $5.5 million and offer low interest rates. Another interesting feature is that repayment terms can extend as long as twenty-five years, but ten years is the standard repayment term length.

Some items you will need when applying for an SBA loan: at least two years of business history, a credit score greater than 640 for the business owner, and around $100,000 in annual revenue for your business.

When searching out an SBA loan, look for lenders who are preferred by the SBA, meaning the SBA has chosen these particular lenders over other institutions that deal with SBA loans. If a particular lender does not advertise that they are preferred, simply ask, and they will tell you. The process of an SBA loan seems to go more quickly with a preferred lender. Under the Preferred Lenders program, the SBA gives select lenders more authority to process, close, service, and liquidate SBA-guaranteed loans.

In making its decision, the SBA considers the following factors about the lender:

- Can they process, close, service, and liquidate loans?

- Can they develop and analyze complete loan packages?

- Do they have a satisfactory SBA performance?

If you don't qualify for an SBA loan today, it doesn't mean you can never qualify for one in the future. If you improve your personal credit, get more business history under your belt, and grow your business, you can graduate to an SBA loan in the future.

I mentioned above that there are two SBA loan programs, the 504 and the 7(a).

It's nice to have choices, but then you need to decide which loan is best for you. We will begin with the 504 program.

Question: What is the 504 loan program?

Answer: The SBA 504 loan program is a powerful economic development loan program that offers small businesses another avenue for business financing. It derives its name from Section 504 of the Small Business Investment Act of 1958 (someone is going to want to know that).

The 504 loan program provides approved small businesses with long-term, fixed-rate financing used to acquire fixed assets for expansion or modernization. 504 loans are made available through certified development companies (CDCs), the SBA's community-based partners for providing 504 loans.

About CDCs

A certified development company (CDC) is a nonprofit corporation that promotes economic development within its community through 504 loans. CDCs are certified and regulated by the SBA and work with the SBA and participating lenders (typically banks) to provide financing to small businesses.

504 Loan Eligibility

To be eligible for an SBA 504 loan, a small business must meet the following eligibility requirements:

- The business must be a for-profit, non-publicly traded company.
- Ownership must comprise 51% United States citizens or registered aliens with a green card.
- The business must do business in the United States or its territories.
- The business must be a sole proprietorship, partnership, limited liability company, or corporation.
- The business must occupy at least 51% of the space to be purchased.
- The business's tangible net worth cannot exceed $15 million.
- The business's average net income after federal income taxes (excluding carryover losses) for the two full fiscal years prior to application cannot exceed $5 million.

- Loans cannot be made to businesses engaged in speculation or investment in rental real estate.

504 Loan Benefits for the Small Business

The 504 loan program offers small businesses both immediate and long-term benefits so business owners can focus on growing their businesses.

- **Ninety-percent (90%) Loan-to-Cost Financing**

  This preserves more capital, which you can use to grow your business.

- **Long-Term Below-Market Fixed Interest Rates**

  This saves on interest expenses.

- **Longer Loan Amortizations**

  This has less impact on business cash flow.

- **No Balloon Payments, Calls, or Covenants**

  This gives you more control and more peace of mind.

- **Close within Sixty Days**

  Start enjoying the benefits of commercial property ownership as soon as possible.

- **Assumable Loans**

  SBA 504 loans are always assumable.

504 Loan Structure

504 loans are typically structured with the SBA providing 40% of the total project costs, a participating lender covering up to 50% of the total project costs, and the borrower contributing 10% of the project costs (your down payment). This structure makes it possible for small business owners to own commercial real estate with less money down and get longer-term fixed interest rates than conventional financing methods allow. **Does this mean you have to obtain two loans—one for 50% and one for 40%?** No, your loan broker will wrap everything into a nice, neat package for you. That is what they are there for.

How 504 Loan Funds May Be Used

Proceeds from 504 loans must be used for fixed assets (and certain soft costs) like the following:

- purchase of existing buildings

- purchase of land and land improvements, including grading, street improvements, utilities, parking lots, and landscaping

- construction of new facilities or modernizing, renovating, or converting existing facilities

- purchase of long-term machinery

The Bottom Line: The SBA 504 loan preserves capital and maximizes cash flow for small business owners. It really is the smart choice for small business owners who want to own commercial real estate. Always see if your current business bank has an SBA loan program and get the details. If not, contact a mortgage broker and start asking questions. You'll soon learn a lot.

Of course, you could also speak to a knowledgeable commercial real estate broker, who can likely refer you to clients who have gone through the process and could share their real-life experiences with you.

Question: What is an SBA 7(a) loan?

Answer: An SBA 7(a) loan is a financial tool designed by the Small Business Administration (SBA) to get money into the hands of small business owners.

Running a small business can be tough, especially in times of uncertainty and loss of revenue. One port in the storm could be an SBA loan. In times of hardship, this "do everything" loan could help you get back on your feet. These loans can be used to acquire business essentials like real estate, equipment, working capital, and inventory.

When you apply for an SBA 7(a) loan, you work with a lender, and the SBA participates by guaranteeing a portion of the loan amount. This guarantee from a government agency helps businesses acquire funds, even if they may not have otherwise qualified for a business loan.

The term "7(a) loan" is a catch-all term that refers to more than half a dozen different types of SBA 7(a) loans. Each loan is designed to meet a different need. Here, we will concentrate on using an SBA 7(a) loan for the purchase of real estate.

SBA 7(a) Eligibility Requirements

The SBA rarely specifies what businesses are eligible. Rather, the agency outlines what businesses are *not* eligible. However, there are some universal requirements. So, if you're looking for support from the SBA, they've got some requirements you'll need to make sure you meet:

- You must be officially registered as a for-profit business, and you must be operating legally.

- Your business must have fewer than 500 employees and less than $7.5 million in revenue on average each year for the past three years.

- Your net income must be under $5 million (after taxes and not counting carryover losses), and your tangible net worth must be less than $15 million.

- You must show you're investing your own time and money in the business, having "invested equity."

- Your business must be physically based in the United States, and you must do business with the United States and its territories.

- You'll need to prove you've got a sound business purpose for the loan you're requesting and that your intended funds usage is approved by the SBA.

- You must use alternative financial resources, including personal assets, before seeking financial help.

- You will need to prove you're not delinquent on any existing debts to the United States government (e.g., taxes or student loans).

Additional Beneficial Business Qualities

There are a few additional qualities that can increase your likelihood of being approved for an SBA 7(a) loan:

- a good credit score (preferably above 680)

- a history free from recent bankruptcies, foreclosures, or tax liens

- a business that has been operating for at least two years

- the ability to make a down payment of 10% if your intended use of funds is to purchase a business, commercial real estate, or business-related equipment

- sufficient cash flow to meet your debt obligations

- sufficient working capital (once you subtract liabilities from assets)

- "good character" according to the SBA (partially based on your track record of managing your resources and day-to-day business affairs)

Be aware that the eligibility requirements are an art, not an exact science, so the best thing to do if you are unsure whether you qualify for an SBA loan is to speak to an SBA loan officer and ask. They can be very helpful.

Ineligible Businesses

A business must be engaged in an activity the SBA deems acceptable to qualify for financial assistance from a federal provider. The following businesses are not eligible for assistance because of the activities they conduct:

- financial businesses primarily engaged in the business of lending, such as banks, finance companies, payday lenders, etc.

- businesses owned by developers and landlords who do not actively use or occupy the assets acquired or improved with the loan proceeds (sorry, real estate investors)

- businesses located in a foreign country (businesses in the United States owned by foreigners may qualify)

- speculative businesses (such as oil exploration)

7(a) Loan Benefits for a Small Business

Some of the 7(a) loan benefits for a small business include:

- flexible structure

- up to 90% financing

- lower down payment compared to other financing options

- lower monthly payments

- variable and fixed rates

- loan terms of five to twenty-five years

- five- to seven-year term for working capital

- up to ten years' amortization for business acquisition or equipment financing

- up to twenty-five years' amortization for real estate

- soft costs such as goodwill, franchise fees, and closing costs are eligible to be paid for by this loan

The SBA will make a loan based on the "value" of the business, even if the collateral does not add up to 100% of the loan amount. In some cases, they will fund deals with no hard collateral too.

Due to the loan being largely guaranteed, a bank will take on a type of asset they might normally avoid. Some examples of these higher-risk businesses include hotels, restaurants, and gas stations.

7(a) Loan Structure

The stated purpose of SBA 7(a) loans is to encourage lenders to provide fair loans to businesses that might otherwise be unable to obtain funding on reasonable terms and conditions. The term "7(a) loan" comes from Section 7(a) of the Small Business Act of 1953, which first authorized the SBA to both provide and guarantee loans to small businesses in the United States. (You know I had to add that in, right?)

Once a business owner finds an SBA-approved lender they want to work with, they can begin the process of obtaining an SBA loan. Most SBA 7(a) loans allow businesses to borrow up to $5 million. The SBA will guarantee 85% of loans up to $150,000 and 75% of loans greater than $150,000.

The SBA sets a maximum interest rate, but you and your lender can negotiate within that limit. Interest rates are based on the prime rate, the size of the loan, and the maturity of the loan. In addition to caps on interest rates, SBA loans also protect businesses from certain fees. However, SBA loans also come with prepayment penalties that cover the first three years of the loan.

How 7(a) Loan Funds May Be Used

7(a) loan funds may be used to:

- acquire land (by purchase or lease)

- improve a site (e.g., grading, streets, parking lots, and landscaping)

- purchase one or more existing buildings

- convert, expand, or renovate one or more existing buildings

- construct one or more new buildings

- acquire (by purchase or lease) and install fixed assets, including furniture, fixtures, machinery, and equipment

- purchase inventory, supplies, and raw materials

- finance working capital, including permanent and revolving working capital

Quick Thought: An easy place to get started finding out information about SBA loans is the bank you currently use. They may have loan programs that you can consider (or compare). If not, they can recommend some local banks to contact.

The SBA 504 Loan vs. the SBA 7(a) Loan

	SBA 504 LOAN (Commercial Real Estate & Equipment) 90% Fixed-Rate	SBA 7(a) LOAN (General Purpose)
LOAN SIZE	Minimum: $125,000 Maximum: $20 million+	Minimum: $50,000 Maximum: $5 million
INTEREST RATE	• Fixed	• Predominantly variable with some fixed-rate options
TERMS	• 25 years (real estate) • 20 years (real estate) • 10 years (equipment)	• Up to 25 years (real estate) • Up to 10 years (business acquisition and equipment) • 5 to 7 years (working capital) • Weighted average for mixed-use requests
DOWN PAYMENT	• 10% borrower	• Minimum 10% borrower (often more)
ELIGIBLE BUSINESS SIZE	• Business net worth not to exceed $15 million • Average net profit after taxes for 2 consecutive years not to exceed $5 million	• Determined by industry type • Annual sales not to exceed range of $750,000 to $33.5 million for retail, service, and agriculture • Number of employees not to exceed range of 100 to 1,000 for wholesale and manufacturing

	SBA 504 LOAN (Commercial Real Estate & Equipment) 90% Fixed-Rate	SBA 7(a) LOAN (General Purpose)
LOAN STRUCTURE	• 50% bank loan • 40% CDC loan • 10% borrower down payment	• Loan structure negotiable (dependent on risk) • 10% down payment (minimum)
PROCEEDS' USE	• Purchase existing building • Acquire land and begin ground-up construction (can include soft cost development fees) • Expand existing building • Finance building improvements • Purchase equipment	• Expand, acquire, or start a business • Purchase or construct real estate • Refinance existing business debt • Buy equipment • Provide working capital • Construct leasehold improvements • Purchase inventory
PROGRAM REQUIREMENTS	• 51% owner occupancy for existing building • 60% owner occupancy for new construction • Equipment must have a minimum 10-year economic life	• 51% owner occupancy for existing building • 60% owner occupancy for new construction • All assets financed must be used for the direct benefit of the business

	SBA 504 LOAN (Commercial Real Estate & Equipment) 90% Fixed-Rate	**SBA 7(a) LOAN** (General Purpose)
COLLATERAL	• Generally, project assets being financed are used as collateral • Personal guaranties by the principal owners of 20% or more ownership are required	• Subject assets acquired by loan proceeds • Pledge of personal residence unless bank can justify why that is unnecessary • Personal guaranties by the principal owners of 20% or more ownership are required
FEES	• Fees are financed in the 504 loan • Fees are negotiated for the 50% bank loan • Servicing fee (lowest allowed by SBA) for CDC plus a legal review fee	• Fees can be financed in the 7(a) loan • Fees vary with the size of the loan paired with the 504 loan • Additional 0.25% charged on any loan portion above $1 million

Question: What is the "green" provision of an SBA loan?

Answer: Small business entrepreneurs are discovering other advantages of SBA 504 financing, including the "green" provision, which allows higher lending amounts for small business owners who want to buy or improve commercial or industrial buildings to make them more energy efficient.

To qualify for the "green" provision, small business owners need to demonstrate a projected 10% reduction in energy costs by implementing one or more energy-saving improvements (e.g., insulation, energy-efficient lighting, more efficient heating/air conditioning, etc.).

Question: What is a bridge loan? Why would I need a bridge loan?

Answer: Bridge loans are temporary loans secured by your existing facility or other real estate. These loans can fill the gap between the sales price of a new property and the buyer's new mortgage in the event the buyer's existing property has not sold before escrow closes on the new property. You are effectively borrowing the down payment on the new property.

Also, a commercial real estate loan may take longer to complete, and the property you are purchasing needs to be purchased prior to the approval of your loan. Some institutions or individuals will make you a temporary loan to purchase your new property with the understanding that you will pay them back when you obtain your original loan.

Because they are funded so quickly and the demand or need for them is crucial to a buyer, the lender of a bridge loan can charge a much higher interest rate. This is why it's important to weigh the benefits and drawbacks of a bridge loan to decide if it makes sense for you.

Question: What are the tax benefits that come with investing in real estate?

Answer: When you own real estate as an investment or as your place of business operation, you are entitled to many more tax benefits or tax deductions than when you own a residential home. Investment real estate is treated differently than a residential home that you live in.

<u>The tax advantages/tax deductions are as follows:</u>

First, any income that you earn from renting or leasing your investment property is defined as taxable income. Before being taxed on that income, you can deduct all the expenses incurred on that property:

- property taxes
- depreciation of the property
- property assessments
- city or county licenses and fees
- the cost of property insurance
- the cost of landscape maintenance
- the cost of building repairs
- property management fees
- accounting fees related to the property
- legal fees related to the property
- interest on the mortgage payment
- bank fees related to the property
- commissions or fees paid to real estate brokers for leasing the property
- travel expenses to monitor your investment property

Many buyers of commercial property purchase the property and hold title in their own name and lease the property to their business. This is a powerful tax strategy for commercial property owners.

Question: I'm looking to buy a building, and I have two or three brokers conducting a search for me. If one misses something, the other one will find it, right?

Answer: That depends. I have found the more brokers a buyer has looking for them, the less that buyer will actually see. If a broker knows a buyer is working with other brokers, they will put in less effort because there is no definite reward for their work.

Interview at least two or three commercial brokers, decide which one you would like to have represent your best interests, and use them exclusively. You can then be assured that the broker is knowledgeable and in your corner when it comes to finding, researching, and making offers on the appropriate commercial property.

If the broker knows you are using them exclusively, they can announce to the rest of the brokerage community that they represent a client looking to purchase a particular property, and other brokers can contact your broker to make them aware of those off-market opportunities.

If you and your exclusive broker are not getting along, or you do not believe they are representing your best interests, you can always fire them and hire another broker.

True Story

Early in my career, I was representing a well-known company looking to purchase commercial property all around the state of California. I had found a location for them that they were very enthusiastic about. We made an offer on the property, and the property was placed in escrow almost immediately. The escrow was for a six-month period with a $100,000 deposit from the buyer becoming nonrefundable after ninety days.

On day ninety, the $100,000 deposit became nonrefundable. This was a good indication that, so far, the escrow was favorable to the buyer and had a great likelihood of closing. (You don't let $100,000 go nonrefundable unless there is a great likelihood of closing the escrow.)

On day 179 of the 180-day escrow, I received an envelope from the escrow company. Thinking the escrow may have closed a day early, I excitedly opened up the escrow package. However, inside the envelope was an escrow cancellation letter.

The day before escrow was supposed to close, the buyer decided not to buy the property and walked away from $100,000. It happens.

Question: Why should I go to the city or county before I make a purchase or lease offer on a commercial property?

Answer: If you're going to purchase a commercial property or be the tenant in a property with a net lease, you'll be paying all of the expenses. The last thing you want is to be surprised by any of the government expenses that regularly occur with a particular commercial property.

Additional expenses beyond the mortgage payment that an owner or a tenant on a net lease would be responsible for include property taxes, common area maintenance (CAM) charge, property insurance, landscape maintenance, building or property maintenance, and, of course, any property assessments imposed by the county or city. Once the entire financial outlay is known, you can get a much better handle on the total expense for that particular property.

Other reasons for going to the city before purchasing or leasing a property would be to see the city's general plan for the area that the property is located in. Do they have special incentives that you could take advantage of? Are there any special fines assessed for that area? Are you able to obtain electricity at a lower cost in a certain area? Does the city have any plans for the surrounding area regarding redevelopment, city projects, etc.?

You should also ask the city or county if your type of business is acceptable at the particular location of interest, acceptable with a conditional use permit, or prohibited. It's well worth an hour or two of your time to get as much knowledge about your future location as possible because this might save you time, trouble, and money in the future.

Question: What is a cap rate?

Answer: A commercial real estate cap rate (which is short for capitalization rate) is the rate of return on investment in commercial real estate based upon the amount of income it's expected to generate. This statistic is generated to help an investor determine the potential return on their investment in the property.

A cap rate is one type of measurement used in evaluating an investment that indicates the risk and the potential rate of return for a prospective property. The commercial real estate cap rate of a property can be determined by taking the annual net operating income and dividing it by the current market value of the property. The net operating income can be determined by looking at the annual return on the property after subtracting any operating costs of the property.

So, John, our example investor, is looking to purchase a building for $900,000. The building brings in $60,000 in income and incurs $15,000 in expenses in a year.

Subtract the annual expenses from the yearly income, and you get the net operating income (NOI). The NOI would then be $45,000 a year in our example. To figure out the cap rate for this building, you simply divide the NOI by the purchase price ($45,000/$900,000 = 5%). The cap rate for John's investment building is 5%. What does that mean?

John's investment cap rate of 5% must be considered in relation to other factors affecting the purchase. A higher percentage is viewed as a high-risk investment bringing in a better return. The lower the rate, the lower the risk involved and the lower the profit capability. However, the cap rate of a property may change over time, with a higher rate bringing in more profits in the future.

A cap rate could mean different things in different situations. Factors that can influence cap rates include location, interest rates, growth, supply vs. demand, property type, rents that are above or below market, the length of the lease term, and the financial strength/credit rating of the tenant.

An investor needs to sift through a great deal of information about a property to determine its possible return on investment, but it's still essential to make the wisest decision when investing your hard-earned money.

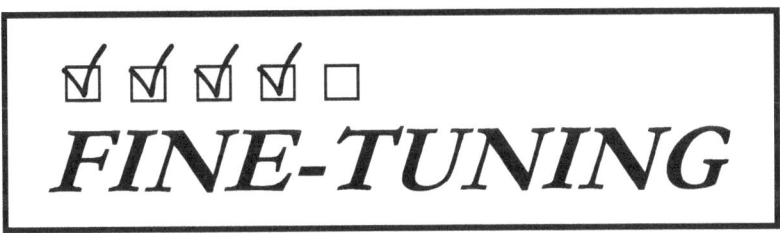

FINE-TUNING

Question: The building I want to buy currently has a tenant occupying it. How can I be sure the property will be vacant when my escrow closes?

Answer: The first thing you want to do to help eliminate this concern is include specific language in the escrow instructions that state the building is to be delivered to you vacant at the close of escrow. That one line in the escrow instructions will ensure that the escrow will not close until the building is vacant.

It's still a good idea for you to stay informed of the tenant's moving plans. You might want to ask the tenant when they plan on leaving and where they will be relocating to, and then keep an eye on the property to see if their moving plans are in line with the date that the escrow is scheduled to close.

Question: What if I am in escrow, but I want to begin construction on tenant improvements or actually begin working inside the building?

Answer: Most sellers will shy away from having their buyer occupy the property prior to escrow closing. This can be a dangerous proposition for the seller because if the buyer does not close escrow, the buyer can become a tenant at sufferance. The seller would then have to begin an eviction process to have the buyer, now the tenant, vacate the building if the tenant does not cooperate and leave the property.

If you want to begin doing your business inside the building, you might consider entering into a lease as the seller's tenant until your escrow closes. If, for some reason, escrow does not close, the lease could continue to be in effect, and you would be able to occupy the building legally. Typically, these kinds of leases have a hefty lease rate as an incentive for the buyer/tenant to complete the escrow. After all, the owner wants to sell the building, not continue to be a landlord.

Sometimes lease rates can be twice, three times, even up to five times the normal market rent per month—an outrageous sum if you were to continue the lease. This situation ultimately forces you to either continue leasing the property for an outrageous amount of money or find some way to close the escrow.

If you want to enter the premises during escrow to survey and do some measuring to help determine where you can place equipment, products, office space, etc., that is allowed during the escrow, as long as you notify the seller of your entry into the premises.

Question: What is a preliminary title report, and how much attention should I pay to it?

Answer: A preliminary title report (PTR) is a document prepared by a title company on real property once an escrow has opened.

If you have a relationship with a commercial real estate broker, usually that broker can obtain a PTR for you. A PTR provides all kinds of information about a property that is essential for a buyer to know, including how title in a property is currently held and what kinds of exceptions to title may exist, such as easements, liens, and encumbrances. The PTR then becomes the final title report on which title insurance is based.

In addition to specific exceptions to title, the title report will also list standard exclusions from coverage. In virtually every real estate transaction, the buyer has the right to approve or object to the preliminary title report and cancel the deal unless the seller can provide clean title by eliminating certain exceptions to title prior to the closing of escrow. But a buyer may only have a short period of time in which to review and take appropriate action if there are any unacceptable exceptions to title.

If you are unsure about any title exceptions, ask your real estate broker or hire a real estate attorney.

Question: How do I find out if I'm getting good title to the property?

Answer: Good title, sometimes referred to as clear title, means that the ownership interest in a particular piece of real property is free and clear from liens, litigations, and claims (except for annual property tax liens imposed by the government and utility easements).

Clear title is necessary before the property is sold; otherwise, the buyer may risk a third party emerging and claiming that the seller did not have full ownership of the parcel and a claim or lien on the property still exists. It is important for you to discuss the preliminary title report with your commercial real estate broker and the title officer who has issued the title report. If there are any further questions or concerns, it is never a bad idea to consult an attorney specializing in real estate law.

Question: Does it matter how I take title to the property I am purchasing?

Answer: There are many issues that can arise with respect to how you take title to real property, especially with commercial property. If you take title as an individual, you may expose yourself to potential liability. You could also take title through a business, most likely a corporation or a limited liability company (LLC). This could limit your potential liability.

If you have joint ownership, you should clearly understand the difference between taking title as joint tenants, tenants in common, a partnership, or community property. You should also clearly understand your rights versus the rights of your co-owners or partners. Each of these types of ownership has significant ownership implications and rights of survivorship. It's always advisable to seek professional advice, including from your attorney and CPA, to help you make a smart decision regarding taking title to real property.

Question: I just received a title report. There is a lot here that I don't understand. Who can help?

Answer: As previously mentioned, you can ask your commercial real estate broker. But without a doubt, the best resource is the title officer who issued the title report. As always, be sure to employ the services of a competent real estate attorney.

Question: In buying commercial real estate for my business, do I need to get an environmental site assessment?

Answer: The short answer is yes, and the long answer is yes.

There are situations where it definitely makes sense to get an environmental site assessment, such as when you are buying a service station or manufacturing business. If the chance of finding any problems seems remote, should you skip an expensive assessment? You're probably doing yourself a disservice if you don't get one, as any problem that arises could result in catastrophic liability exposure for you, even if you didn't cause the problem.

There are different types of environmental site assessments. Phase 1 involves an inspection of the property and a review of various records but does not actually involve excavating, drilling, or testing soil or water samples. These activities are usually done during a Phase 2 assessment, which can be expensive. It's usually advisable for a buyer to do a Phase 1 assessment and consider the results and recommendations before deciding whether to proceed with a Phase 2 assessment.

Hazardous waste environmental contamination can be one of the biggest concerns when owning commercial property. A property owner is responsible for remedying such problems, even if the current property owner did not cause them. This is why it's important not to purchase real property without first obtaining a Phase 1, and, if necessary, a Phase 2 environmental report. These problems may not be obvious or apparent to the naked eye and could arise from anything ranging from a leaking underground storage tank to a previous occupant pouring paint down a hole on the property.

If you are in the chain of title of contaminated property, even if you owned the property years ago, you could still be responsible for cleaning up the property if it can be established that you were the source or cause of the hazardous waste. And the cost of an environmental cleanup operation can run into the thousands.

I remember hearing about an owner of an eight-story office building who literally walked away from ownership of the building because the environmental cleanup costs were more than the building was worth. This was an office building with more than 60,000 square feet.

Question: Does "as is" really mean "as is"?

Answer: "As is" essentially means the seller is offering a piece of real property with no warranties as to its quality. Buyers can assume that the property might have some issues that the seller does not want to deal with or face negotiation or demands for repairs for. A seller might be trying to evade liability by selling a property "as is."

Many states have legislation to prevent a seller from completely passing the buck on certain issues, such as environmental cleanup, hazardous waste disposal, or other dangerous conditions. The law sometimes requires mandatory disclosure of defective conditions or problems with the property being sold.

For example, a seller would likely be found liable if real property were sold to a buyer and the seller failed to disclose that the foundation was buckling. Bottom line: any time real property is being sold "as is," enter into it with your eyes wide open.

Question: How much is commercial real estate taxed? Is it the same as residential?

Answer: The amount of taxes levied on commercial real estate all depends on the location of the real estate. Each county will have a particular base tax rate on the property. This is true whether it is commercial real estate or residential real estate.

Government agencies that have jurisdiction require business and property owners to fill out tax forms to provide information about the rental income if it is an investment property. The variables that impact the amount of taxes you will have to pay for your commercial property can include the following: income generated from the property, property expenses, location of the property, and more. Commercial real estate taxes can change drastically based on many different variables. So, it isn't possible to provide an exact answer, as the response will depend on you, the property, and the location of the property.

Beyond what the county might assess on a property, a city may also impose additional taxes, bonds, levies, or fees that can be placed upon the entire city, a particular section of the city, a particular street in the city, or a particular property.

In addition to base county taxes, your tax bill may include an additional fee for schools or the water district or special assessment charges such as a mosquito or vector control charge or a sewer user fee. The list goes on and on, depending on how creative a municipality can get with fees.

In general, the taxes for residential property and commercial property are quite similar, the exception being that there is a greater chance of additional assessments on commercial property, but these won't necessarily be very expensive.

Prior to purchasing a property or leasing a property on a triple net lease, it might be beneficial to ask the current property holder for a copy of previous years' secured property tax bills. In the property tax bill, it will show the basic tax levy rate in addition to any other assessments. You can also get this information at the county assessor's office.

True Story

Have you heard of chasing the market? Here is a textbook example of it.

I had a client whom I will call Eddie. Eddie saw his friend (also my client) purchase a few industrial buildings, and his friend had created enormous wealth from the increase in their value. Eddie wanted to do the same thing, so he asked me to look for a good industrial building for him to purchase and operate his business in. I showed him a building that seemed to work perfectly for his business; the purchase price was $85 per square foot.

Eddie told me that $85 per square foot was $10 per square foot more than many of the buildings he had seen sell in the area. I told him this property had frontage on a main street; a large, fenced yard providing the storage he would need; and a perfect location, which meant the building would likely increase in value. Unable to get comfortable with the asking price, Eddie passed on it.

About a year later, Eddie telephoned and asked me again to look for a building for his business. I found a great property, but the market had increased, and this building was $115 per square foot. Even though he liked the building, he thought it was too expensive and asked me to look for other buildings. I did, but the asking price was only a few dollars less, and the property was just not quite as good as the original one I had shown him. In only a few days, the building sold, and Eddie had lost out again. This happened two more times within a year, with similar results.

About three years later, Eddie again asked me to look for a building for him to purchase. This time, I found a fantastic corner building on a major street with all the amenities he needed and wanted. The asking price was $140 per square foot, but I was very confident that I could get the building for him for $135 per square foot.

Eddie said he wanted to get the best price, and he wanted me to submit a very low offer on the property. I protested, telling him he would ruin his chances of buying it. In one week, it was in escrow with another buyer for $140 per square foot, and Eddie had missed out again.

True Story continues . . .

True Story continued . . .

> Years later, Eddie called me up again and asked what buildings were selling for these days. "About $200 to $225 per square foot," I told him. There was silence on the other end of the line. Finally, Eddie said, "Well, if you find any good deals out there, let me know."
>
> As I hung up the phone, I leaned back in my chair and said to myself, "Don't sit by the phone waiting for my call."

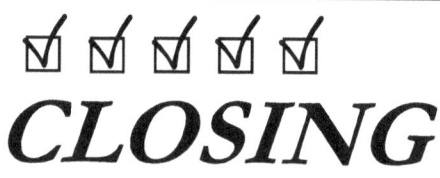

CLOSING

Question: How much are the escrow fees, and who pays them—the buyer or the seller?

Answer: A rough calculation for the cost of escrow is two dollars for every thousand dollars of the sales price, plus $250. So, if a property sold for $1 million, the escrow fee is roughly $2,250. But just know there are as many "formulas" for obtaining an escrow fee as there are escrow companies. Most escrow companies charge around the same amount. But it doesn't hurt to ask the escrow company for a discount on the fees. Often, they will reduce their cost, and you may have a good chance of saving a few hundred dollars.

Most purchase contracts state that the escrow fees are divided equally between the buyer and the seller. Make sure that the escrow company being used has experience in handling commercial property.

Question: Besides the cost of escrow, what other fees am I responsible for as the buyer of a real property?

Answer: There are many other expenses beyond the basic escrow costs. Below, you will find some of those expenses/closing costs.

On the buyer's side, closing costs usually include loan origination fees, discount points on the loan, appraisal fees, environmental studies, recording fees, and taxes. Some miscellaneous costs might include special title searches, surveys, credit report changes, notary fees, and delivery costs.

It is the seller's responsibility to pay for title insurance.

Question: Is there a checklist of items I need to be aware of if I'm buying a property? I don't want to forget anything.

Answer: There are some escrow companies that will give you an escrow checklist precisely, so you don't forget anything. Another source for your checklist is the actual purchase offer. In the purchase offer, there is a list of contingencies that the sale of the property is based upon. These include, but are not limited to, a property inspection, the condition of title, and environmental reports. You can list these contingencies as your "checklist."

It's also important that you surround yourself with knowledgeable, professional, and experienced people during your purchase. From the commercial real estate broker to the title and escrow officer and real estate attorney, use the best. If you are surrounded by the best support team, the chances of you forgetting anything diminish to almost zero. The best people do not cost that much more than average people, and you want to have the best results possible.

Question: My escrow to purchase the building is due to close tomorrow, and there are still a number of repairs the seller was going to make as a condition of closing the escrow, but the repairs have not been made. What do I do now?

Answer: Immediately contact the escrow company stating that you don't want the escrow to close unless certain repairs have been made. If this conflicts with your loan and you cannot delay the escrow in order to have the repairs made, then you might consider escrow instructions that state that a certain amount of money will be held in escrow equivalent to the cost of the repairs, and it will only be released to the seller when the repairs are made.

This may give you the leverage you need with the seller to get these repairs done as soon as possible or reach an agreement to your satisfaction that will allow the escrow to close on time.

Quick Thought: When closing an escrow, try to close it on a Monday or Tuesday. That way, you will have business days after the close of escrow to obtain keys and other vital items that can help you with your move. If you close on a Friday, you might have to wait for keys and other items until Monday or Tuesday of the next week; meanwhile, you're paying the interest on a new loan over Saturday and Sunday without any benefit.

Question: How soon after the sale closes can I sell or refinance my building?

Answer: That depends on the type of penalty you want to incur. Most loans have a prepayment penalty of a certain percentage of the loan. However, that penalty is typically reduced annually until there is no penalty. Generally, the prepayment penalty on most loans expires after five years. Also, government loans such as SBA loans may have additional penalties if you try to sell or refinance the property within one year of purchase. You should always know what the prepayment penalty is for any loan you enter into.

The best reason to refinance or sell a property so soon after purchase would be that the increase in value you would receive from the sale would more than pay for the penalty you would incur.

CHAPTER **3** THREE

"Landlords grow rich in their sleep."

— John Stuart Mill

I Am an Owner Who Wants to Lease My Property

You are the owner of an industrial building, and you know that you do not want to sell; you want to lease. You are prepared to be a landlord and handle all that comes with it, including managing and maintaining the property. Included on that list are the *benefits* of being a landlord: the increase in property value over time, the depreciation of the building to offset income, the monthly income from the rent check hitting your mailbox on the first of the month (as long as your tenant is current). Some call it "mailbox money."

Receiving passive income is fantastic. Let's break that down: *passive* is easy to do, and *income* is great! To be able to rely on that monthly passive income, you will need to gather all of the best information possible so you can attract and obtain a financially fit tenant to occupy your facility at the highest lease rate possible. If you lease your property to a tenant who does not pay the rent regularly or has other difficulties, then you have neither passive nor income!

It has been proven time and time again that even after paying a commission, if you use the services of an experienced and knowledgeable commercial real estate broker, you will most likely obtain:

- a more financially fit tenant

- a longer lease term

- a higher lease rate

- a more highly valued property

Let's start building your knowledge of leasing by getting your questions and concerns answered.

Question: I want to lease my property. What's the first thing I should do?

Answer: Unless you are a professional real estate broker, a property manager, or someone who deals with commercial real estate transactions on a daily basis, seek professional help.

The largest asset of many property owners is their commercial real estate, and in an effort to save pennies on a real estate broker, they forfeit thousands of dollars in the process. Do not let this next story happen to you.

True Story

I was out cold-calling on a street with industrial buildings on either side of the road and walked into the office of a man who looked like he was the owner of the business and the building. I asked if there was anything I could do to help him with any of his real estate needs. He said, "No, thank you," and he proudly stated that he had leased his building next door to a new tenant just last week. I congratulated him and asked for the particulars of the transaction so I could apprise myself of the deals happening in the area.

(You know what's coming next, don't you?)

He said he had just signed a five-year lease with the new tenant for $0.58 per square foot, gross. This was an entire $0.10 per square foot more than he had been getting from his previous tenant. I told him it was good that the rent had been increased, but he was still under the market by about $0.15 per square foot.

This turned out to be about a $2,250-a-month mistake. And over the course of the next five years, this mistake mushroomed to $235,000, not including annual increases.

I have seen owners make this mistake time after time. Once, it cost an owner over $1 million! He had taken advice from friends and boasted to me that he hadn't had to pay a real estate commission or an attorney. I was about to explain why he should have, but I didn't have the heart to tell him, and it wouldn't have changed the final outcome anyway.

The true story above is why you should seek professional help and employ the use of a commercial real estate broker who can maximize your commercial real estate asset to its fullest.

Dan hit the streets cold calling

Question: Should I use a real estate agent to lease my property?

Answer: You don't need to know everything about leasing your property if you hire a real estate professional who does. Henry Ford once said that when you hire people who are smarter than you are, it proves you're smarter than they are.

By hiring a professional commercial real estate broker, you'll have someone on your team who has a great deal of education and experience in the particular area in which your property is located. A professional agent will reduce the likelihood of frivolous showings to unqualified or unrealistic tenants and filter out all those phone calls that lead nowhere.

Agents have intimate knowledge of the area your property is located in and can identify comparable lease transactions of consequence and meaning. You can go down to the county records office and find out what a property has *sold* for, but rarely will you ever be able to know what a commercial property has *leased* for. This is extremely important information if you want to lease your property. Professional real estate agents know the market conditions in your area and have an entire network of other agents they have done business with in the past whom they can speak to and get the real dirt on how and why a transaction occurred.

Hiring a real estate agent will also get your property into the various multiple listing services that are so valuable in today's marketplace. Professional real estate agents have access to lessees, so using a real estate agent gives you access to their network of highly qualified tenants.

Receiving guidance on what to be aware of is another benefit of using a professional real estate agent. They will be on top of the latest rules, regulations, and laws when it comes to leasing commercial property and the types of tenants who are allowed in your building. Professional real estate agents also have negotiation skills and can distance themselves from the emotional aspects of a transaction. Real estate professionals keep client information confidential from competing interests as well.

According to an internal Lee & Associates Commercial Real Estate Services, Inc., survey, broker-listed property received an 18% higher lease rate than properties leased by owners without a real estate broker. Finding a tenant who wants to lease your building is relatively easy, but finding the right tenant can be much more difficult. Brokers will find you good tenants. The correct lessee can maximize your bottom line by reducing costs and ensuring that you enjoy a steady stream of rental income without the headache.

A professional real estate agent might cost you a 5% or 6% commission to find a financially fit tenant, but you will more than make up that cost with the added benefit of a higher-quality tenant, a longer lease term, a higher rental income, and a sound lease document that protects you and your rights.

Question: Can I get a reduction on the commission? Don't all you brokers do the same thing?

Pre-Answer: "If you pay peanuts, you get monkeys." — Chinese Proverb

Answer: Yes, it's possible to reduce a commission, but most good brokers won't reduce their commission because their services are well worth it. A great broker is valuable for their information and past experience.

Some brokers who don't have much experience will take a listing just for the sake of having a listing. Brokers like that are probably not worth the reduced commission you would be paying them anyway.

And no, not all brokers are the same. Some brokers "work" by putting up a "For Sale" sign, publishing a brochure, and waiting for the phone to ring. Other brokers are more proactive and do mailings, create websites, knock on doors (literally), and use the telephone to advertise the availability of your property.

This is why it's imperative for you to interview at least two brokers before listing your property for lease so you can determine what they will do for you.

Question: How do I know if I should lease (or sell) my building?

Answer: This is something that you need to know and understand before listing the property.

If you want to lease a commercial property, you do so because you want to retain ownership of the property and enjoy the monthly income that investment provides. But what if you don't want the headaches that sometimes come with ownership? The perfect solution is a professional property manager. Always ask your commercial real estate broker for a referral to a property manager, as they deal with them constantly and can tell you who is good and who to steer away from.

If you want to sell commercial real estate, you do so for one of two reasons: (1) you found another opportunity where the total purchase price of the new property can benefit you more than your existing property; (2) you don't want the responsibility that comes with ownership.

Whatever you decide, your wisest course of action is to seek advice and understanding from as many qualified professional individuals as possible, including a certified public accountant.

Question: How are commercial real estate professionals paid for their services when completing a lease?

Answer: Most of us know that when a property is sold, the real estate broker's service fee (commission) is usually 5% or 6% of the sales price. But what is a real estate broker's commission on a lease?

Commercial real estate agents receive a commission upon the signing of a lease between an owner and a tenant. The amount of the commission is usually calculated as a percentage of the lease value and ranges between 5% and 6%. For instance, if a tenant signs a three-year lease for a 2,000-square-foot building at $1.00 per square foot/month, the commission is calculated as follows: 2,000 square feet × $1.00 = $2,000 × 12 months = $24,000 × 3 years = $72,000 × 5% = $3,600. So, a 5% commission to the real estate broker would be about $3,600.

The owner of the leased building pays the agent's commission. Typically, the agent receives half on the signing of the lease and the remaining half when the tenant begins occupying the building.

Question: Don't all brokers cooperate with each other and share the commission?

Answer: For the most part, yes; however, there are a few exceptions in the marketplace, and you need to be aware of them.

When you hire a broker to market your property for lease or sale, it's important for you to know if the broker you hire cooperates with other brokers to broadcast your available building to the multitude of other brokers in the marketplace. If a real estate broker doesn't cooperate with other real estate brokers, what motivation would any other broker in the marketplace have to bring a tenant or a buyer to your building? And how would they know that your building is available in the first place?

If you want to sell or lease your property in a timely fashion, you must make sure that the real estate broker you choose to list your property will split the commission fifty-fifty with the real estate broker who brings in the tenant or buyer. It's also very important for your broker to be respected and well-liked by other brokers so there will be an attitude of cooperation and respect among all those involved.

Question: What kind of marketing material will a real estate broker create to market my building?

Answer: That depends on the listing, you (the owner), and the broker.

Depending on the type of listing, a broker can create a simple one-page brochure, an intricate four-page color brochure, or a multipage marketing extravaganza with all the appropriate bells and whistles.

At a minimum, the marketing material the broker prepares should have a color photo of the property, a site plan of the property, a locator map, and a list of the building's amenities and provide all of the contact information a prospective tenant needs to act. Even though we are in the computer age and everyone sends information about properties via email, it's always a good idea to have hard copies of brochures, floor plans, and any other types of information regarding a property so it can be reviewed, written on, copied, or anything else a prospective tenant might do to study a property.

Once a broker has prepared a brochure or other type of marketing material, make sure you review and approve it before it's published. This exercise can help catch errors in the size of the building indicated, the office space, electrical power, or any typo that may have occurred. This is also the time to make changes if you think of other amenities or items that should be in the marketing material. Finally, have another set of eyes look at the finished work. After all, it's your property, and it needs to look its best!

If you have interviewed your broker and asked the correct questions, you should be familiar with all the different types of marketing materials that they will provide.

Question: Why should I use a broker or an agent if I have an attorney?

Answer: A knowledgeable broker who is a vital part of your team is a professional. They have "boots on the ground" and know what transactions have occurred and *why*.

They know how long a property has been on the market and *why*. They know who in the market is searching for a property and *why*. Most importantly, an experienced real estate broker has years of experience doing exactly what you want done with your property: leasing or selling it.

Having a real estate attorney available when needed is a wise move, but such an attorney is likely not in the everyday trenches of the active commercial real estate marketplace. Only an experienced, knowledgeable, and active real estate broker who encounters these situations every day and has completed real-life transactions will have the knowledge you need for the overall good of your project.

I have also been asked . . .

Question: If I hire a real estate broker, why do I need to hire an attorney?

Answer: A real estate broker is a licensed professional who is hired to find a tenant and negotiate the lease. However, a broker is typically not an attorney.

Real estate agents, unless they have a law degree, should never provide legal advice. Separate legal advice from an experienced real estate attorney is typically well worth the additional cost. It's far more cost-effective to hire a lawyer to assist with the transaction, verify the various items, and look over the intricate language of the lease than it is to wait until you are embroiled in an expensive lawsuit.

Question: You brokers get paid too much. Can you work with me on the commission?

Answer: Movie stars get paid too much, professional sports athletes get paid too much, doctors and some attorneys get paid too much. Or do they?

These people are providing a professional service, and in the case of a doctor or attorney, they can save you from additional pain in the future, be it physical or financial. An experienced professional, whether an attorney, a CPA, or a commercial real estate broker, is in the same category.

If your real estate broker has a few years of experience, is knowledgeable and motivated, and can act within the mandated fiduciary relationship and complete your real estate transaction with value added, then the case could be made that some commercial real estate brokers are underpaid for what they do.

How about going to your dentist and saying, "Hey, why don't you reduce the cost of that filling?" Do you think your dentist is going to be as careful with your tooth after being asked to reduce their fee?

You want any professional representative who is skilled and responsible for your financial well-being to be properly compensated for their work. You'll probably only do a few transactions with your commercial real estate agent, but these transactions will endure for a few years or forever. So, this is not where you want to cut corners.

A competent, well-experienced real estate broker can save you much more than the cost of their commission.

Question: I am concerned about only having one agent on my listing instead of a team of two or three. Won't more territory be covered if there are two or three agents working on a listing?

Answer: Having two or three agents on the listing can seem like a good idea at first, and it is a good idea if you are leasing a commercial park with different-sized buildings, such as multi-tenant, midsize, and large facilities. It's also a good idea if you are leasing a mixed-use park comprising retail, office, and industrial units. However, if your property is a single-use facility that will most likely be sold or leased to a single user, one agent is sufficient. Hiring more than one agent in this situation often leads to each team member thinking the other is taking care of a task when no one is, so much less gets done.

A team usually consists of a senior agent brought in to demonstrate experience and dealmaking ability to the owner and less senior agents who often do most of the work. In essence, what the owner sees is not what the owner really gets. With so many team members involved from the start, the agents' natural inclination is to try to find a buyer or tenant without involving an outside broker, thus eliminating the need to split the commission with them. This allows them to obtain twice the fee for selling or leasing the facility.

This hurts the owner because the lack of timely and aggressive marketing to outside agents means less exposure to possible buyers or tenants. With two or three agents involved, there could also be a lack of accountability, a clash of personalities, less reward for effort, scheduling conflicts, and resentment toward team members who aren't doing their fair share of the work. On top of that, there could also be a lack of consensus when it comes to marketing, negotiations, and sale and lease documentation.

It has been my experience when working with another real estate agent on a listing that one member does much more work on the transaction than the other. With one agent involved, there is greater focus on the project, no personality conflicts, no scheduling conflicts, a higher reward for effort, and a higher level of accountability.

Question: This is an important portion of my portfolio. I'm concerned about choosing a broker who will be sincerely concerned for my welfare in the ultimate transaction. How can I be assured of my broker's commitment to my project?

Answer: A broker demonstrates commitment to your project by not working on another competing property while your property is listed with him. Ask your real estate agent to do this.

By hiring a broker, you are putting your real estate and financial affairs in someone else's hands and relinquishing some degree of control. Even though you know you might need outside expertise, it is emotionally discomforting to do so. Your broker should do everything possible to help you eliminate or at least reduce that anxiety.

Telephone calls and regular text or email contact during the marketing period can help. Try to choose a real estate agent who doesn't list property on a mass scale so they can put a sufficient amount of time and effort into selling or leasing your property.

Important Thought

I think it's important for a salesperson to own what they sell.

A Porsche dealer selling Porsches all day long who climbs into a 1984 Toyota at the end of the day just doesn't sound right, does it? How can I expect the people I serve to lease or purchase a commercial building from me if I don't share the same experience? Owning commercial property myself has helped me relate to and connect with my clients because I have the knowledge and authority that can only come from someone who has been there. You have to believe in your product enough to own it yourself. Ask the agent you are interested in hiring if they own commercial real estate.

Question: My building has hazardous waste in the soil. Can I lease it?

Answer: Yes, but it's a good idea to alert the prospective tenant to the environmental condition of the soil and building. I would also recommend that you have a Phase 1 environmental study conducted on your property and, if warranted, a Phase 2 environmental study as well.

This could benefit you in a number of different ways. One, maybe you think your property has hazardous waste, but a study may reveal that it doesn't. Two, it's good to know the magnitude of the environmental contamination situation. Maybe it's not as severe as you thought. Three, if there is the potential for a prospective tenant to generate hazardous substances in the course of their business, it would be beneficial to have a baseline of how much contamination, if any, the property has now. Then, if any additional hazardous waste were generated, you would know exactly who contributed to the pollution and could hold that tenant responsible.

If you have a Phase 1 and Phase 2 environmental study completed, this should be part of the information provided to the tenant so that there is full disclosure on your part and less of a chance of legal repercussions down the road.

Question: What should I do to prepare my property for lease?

Answer: There are a number of things that you can do to prepare your property for leasing. The better your property looks, the more rent you can charge. If there are small things within view that are broken or need to be repaired, a potential tenant is going to think, "If the small things are broken or need to be repaired, then what about the major things like air-conditioning, the roof, the plumbing, and the electrical?" The best thing you can do to eliminate a potential tenant's worries or concerns is to make your facility look as maintained as possible.

Walk through your facility and look at all of the items that a future tenant might see. Do all the overhead doors function? Do all the lights turn on? Does all the plumbing work? Does the air conditioning/heater work? Is the foil insulation on the ceiling hanging down? In short, are there any items that would make a tenant question whether the building has been maintained? At a minimum, everything in the building should function.

One thing you can do to make the biggest positive change to your property with minimal expense is landscaping. Pull up weeds, plant flowers, trim bushes and trees, and make the landscaping look as new and maintained as possible.

Does the outside of the building need painting? This is something that can change the entire look of the property. If the paint is cracked or peeling, if the color is outdated or fading, if there is graffiti or there are stains from a prior tenant, then a new coat of paint can make all the difference. Painting the outside of the building is surprisingly inexpensive for the benefit it will provide. Repaving the asphalt surrounding the building, or at least giving it a quick slurry coat and restriping the parking lot, can make your freshly painted building look virtually new.

It's like donning a shiny pair of shoes with a suit. You wouldn't wear a finely tailored suit with a pair of tennis shoes—or at least you shouldn't if you want to look professional. Even something as simple as washing the windows can make a building look much better by eliminating water spots, dirt, and lime and making them look like new.

What about the inside of the building? As you enter the building, does the front door look old? Is it a wooden door that should be replaced with a glass door? Should it be painted if it's wood or replaced if it's glass? Even something as small as the door handle can send a negative message to a potential tenant if it's broken or in need of repair. Does the front office or reception area need a new coat of paint, a new carpet, or new tile? Does it look tired? All the floors should be clean and stain-free. Replace old carpeting if it doesn't clean up well.

Replace burned-out lightbulbs or entire light fixtures if the style is outdated and not modern. Replace all drop ceiling tiles that are water-stained. Clean all the toilets and sinks in the restrooms, and if they don't clean up well, replace them because sinks and toilets are not very expensive. Paint the interior office walls if the color is faded, outdated, or dirty.

It doesn't cost much to make a building look more inviting, more modern, and free of maintenance issues. More likely than not, you'll be rewarded on the back end.

By having a facility that not only looks maintained but also is maintained, you help limit a future tenant's investigation into the maintenance of the property and its amenities. The future tenant should be focusing on the actual size, the layout, the clearance, and the logistics of the building as it pertains to their business. You need to keep the future tenant's head clear of unimportant items and focused on the overall goal of leasing the building.

Question: The tenant wants me to construct additional improvements, such as offices. I don't know anything about construction. What do I do now?

Answer: Let's say a tenant wants an additional 1,000 square feet of office space in your building. As a commercial building owner, you may not necessarily know how to construct these improvements or know if the city will allow these additional offices. The easiest way to go about this is to contact a building contractor who does this type of improvement. (If your real estate broker is any good, they will be able to recommend experienced contractors.) A general contractor can quickly sketch out some type of office configuration and give you a rough estimate of what these improvements might cost.

For example (this is an easy one), let's say our 1,000 square feet of office space costs $42,000 to construct. If the entire building is 15,000 square feet, and the tenant wants to lease the property for five years (sixty months), the additional monthly rent required to make up for the outlay of $42,000 would be $700 per month ($42,000/60 months = $700 per month).

If the lease rate for the 15,000-square-foot building was $0.85 per square foot, or $12,750 per month, then by adding the additional $700 per month for the new office space, the rent would increase to $13,450 per month, or about $0.895 per square foot. See, that wasn't too painful, was it?

Remember, if you want a return on your $42,000 over a sixty-month period, you might consider charging interest at a rate at least three times the going bank rate. So, if the bank charged a rate of 1.5% interest, you might want to charge 4.5% or 5% on that $42,000 over the five years (a fair return).

Quick Thought: *Many building owners prefer to own industrial buildings and lease them out to tenants because they are "so easy" to lease. Unlike retail or office buildings, where modifying walls and doors, replacing carpets, and reconfiguring HVAC are commonplace, the only thing you have to do to a previously occupied industrial building is "hose it out and lease it up." Often, it's just that easy.*

Question: How can a gardener help me get a higher lease rate?

Answer: If your commercial property doesn't need an exterior paint job or a parking lot slurry coat, consider looking at your landscaping to see if there is room for improvement. Something as simple as trimming the trees can make your property look newer, your building look larger, and the front of your property look more open and inviting to potential tenants.

Just adding flowers to the front of your building, especially around the front entrance, can give the impression that the property is fresh and not old and worn. Also, if you have plants like ivy growing on your building, cut them back and away from the building, and, if necessary, repaint any damaged areas.

In summary, do not let a building become overgrown with trees and plants.

"I didn't use to believe in global warming, but that was before I discovered how to make a profit off it."

Question: What energy-saving items can I install in my building to make it more attractive to potential tenants?

Answer: Install LED lights or the equivalent wherever possible. Save money and save the environment all while reducing the need to change light bulbs frequently.

A 100W incandescent bulb = a 23–30W fluorescent bulb = a 14–20W LED bulb

Check out the table below:

LED vs CFL vs Incandescent Cost	Incandescent	Fluorescent	LED
Watts used	60W	14W	7W
Average cost per bulb	$1	$2	$4 or less
Average lifespan	1,200 hours	8,000 hours	25,000 hours
Bulbs needed for 25,000 hours	21	3	1
Total purchase price of bulbs over 20 years	$42	$12	$8
Cost of electricity (25,000 hours at $0.15 per kWh)	$169	$52	$30
Total estimated cost over 20 years	**$211**	**$54**	**$34**

Question: Are mercury vapor lights being phased out?

Answer: Mercury vapor security lights are being phased out to help protect the environment and promote energy efficiency in lighting. Although the bulbs can still be found, the United States banned the sale of mercury vapor ballasts in 2008.

Quick Thought: Make sure the broker's brochure about your property lists ALL the basic features, including building size, office size clearance, the number and type of loading doors, the presence (or lack thereof) of fire sprinklers, and the amount and type of electrical power. Electrical power is the most common feature to be overlooked and not included in the brochure or the marketing. Don't forget to include this important feature. I've even seen brochures where the address or city wasn't mentioned!

Question: What are some inexpensive energy-saving items I can install in my building to make it more attractive to potential tenants?

Answer: Weatherstripping in the office areas of industrial buildings can help save money by not operating the air conditioner or heater as much. Painting office or warehouse walls a light color will help reflect light within the space and illuminate it much better than darker office walls. Installing foil insulation in warehouse ceilings will help reduce the temperature in the hotter months and also help reflect the light in the warehouse, making it appear brighter. Lighter walls will also tend to make the space seem larger than it is.

On the outside, reflective roof membranes have been shown to lower air conditioning costs by reducing the influx of thermal energy through a roof assembly and into the building. Reflective roofs have also been shown to lower air conditioning loads on buildings, saving energy and money.

If all of the above improvements have been done, this should be mentioned on all marketing materials and whenever potential tenants tour the facility in order to show them the direct benefit a tenant would receive.

Question: The tenant wants to enlarge the ground-level door, install a large ceiling fan, and add electrical service. Should I let them?

Answer: The short answer is yes.

If a tenant wants to add amenities to your building solely at their expense, by all means, let them. You should welcome any improvements to your building that make it more functional, especially on someone else's dime. Just make sure the tenant uses professional contractors and obtains the proper permits and licenses to accomplish all of the agreed-upon work.

If you think the improvements installed by the tenant might be too customized or unsuitable for subsequent tenants, when the tenant vacates the facility, you have the option to demand that they return the space to its original condition.

For example, if the loading door the tenant installed isn't something that would benefit future tenants, you could have that door filled in at the tenant's expense (a larger door is almost always better). The same goes for any other improvements, such as ceiling fans, skylights, or office space.

However, more often than not, a tenant's improvements will increase the overall value of the building.

"A show of hands please...how many of you had the foresight to purchase flood insurance?"

Question: The roof leaks. Sometimes I fix it, and sometimes my tenant fixes it. I really don't know what to do and don't want to bother with it. What should I do?

Answer: The answer to almost every question regarding what should happen when a situation arises, and who should be responsible—especially when it comes to a roof leak—is in the lease document. If you have a net lease, generally speaking, the tenant is responsible for any type of roof maintenance. If you have a gross lease, many times, the landlord is responsible for roof maintenance. You can also have a modified gross or modified net lease, and you and your tenant can determine who will be in charge of maintenance of or repairs to the roof.

The bottom line: if you are a landlord and don't want to bother with the roof, whatever type of lease you have, you can always modify the language of the lease in such a way that the roof maintenance and repair are solely the tenant's responsibility. Just be aware that many tenants will shy away from this, and it may be hard for them to swallow such a directive in the lease. If a tenant is to be responsible for the roof, the tenant will most likely ask for a professional inspection of the roof to detect any maintenance issues and obtain the inspector's opinion on the remaining life of the roof.

STRATEGY

Question: Wait a minute, I'm confused . . . you mean there is a triple net lease, a double net lease, a net lease, a gross lease, an industrial gross lease, *and* a modified gross lease? Which one is right for me?

Answer: If you are the owner of a commercial property and you wish to lease your building, you need to have a written lease signed by you and the lessee before they occupy the property.

When I first got into the business and started talking to owners and tenants, I was amazed at how many tenants occupied a building without a written lease and based on just a handshake.

Nowadays, it's very difficult to find any ongoing handshake deals. With our society becoming more and more litigious, it's imperative to have a written lease to protect yourself and your rights, whether you are a landlord or a tenant.

There are many different types of leases; however, by speaking with an experienced commercial real estate broker, you can identify which lease would be best suited for you and your property.

For practical purposes, I will define two types of leases: the gross lease and the net lease. All other "modified" leases are derivatives of a gross lease or a net lease.

The Gross Lease:

This is a lease in which the tenant pays a specified dollar amount every month to occupy the property. All property taxes and property insurance are paid by the landlord. However, any increases in the property tax or the property insurance over the base year (the first year the tenant occupies the property) are paid by the tenant.

<u>The Net Lease:</u>

With this lease, the tenant pays a specified amount to occupy the property plus *all* other expenses. This includes property tax, property insurance, and any other expense that is levied against the property. Simply speaking, the landlord pays nothing, and the tenant pays everything. These are also commonly called "triple net leases."

Why are net leases sometimes called "triple net leases"? The lease rate is net of taxes, net of insurance, and net of maintenance (the big three or "triple" expenses).

So, which lease is right for you? The majority of industrial leases are gross leases, especially in smaller buildings. Sometimes the market dictates that you offer a gross lease, as it is easier for most tenants to comprehend and limits surprise expenses for the tenants.

For example, a 10,000-square-foot building might have a market lease rate of $0.85 gross per square foot. (I know we didn't say there would be any math involved, but bear with me; this is a pretty good example and doesn't really go beyond fifth-grade math.) This translates to a monthly income of $8,500 per month. From that $8,500, the landlord would pay all the other expenses, including the property taxes and the property insurance. Let's say that all of the expenses, including the property tax, property insurance, and property maintenance, come to $1,000 per month. The landlord receives a net amount of $7,500 per month.

That same 10,000-square-foot building might have a market lease rate of $0.75 triple net per square foot. This adds up to a monthly income of $7,500 per month. However, the landlord does not have to pay the additional expenses of property tax, property insurance, and property maintenance. Those are now the responsibility of the tenant to the tune of $1,000. When all is said and done, the landlord still receives the same $7,500 per month.

There are various reasons to market the property on a gross basis or a net basis depending on the circumstances in the market and the type of tenant that a particular property will attract. It's also true that if you want to be less "hands-on" and not have to manage a property too closely, then some type of net lease might be right for you. This is where your commercial real estate broker can be of great value in helping you determine which type of lease is right for you.

Question: My building has been listed and available on the market for many weeks without much action. Should I change brokers? Should I keep the one I have? What should I do?

Answer: This can happen from time to time. Sometimes a broker becomes complacent or unmotivated to market a property in the way that an owner wishes. There can be a number of reasons why a building may have little or no action.

Ask your existing broker how many transactions there have been for buildings in the area that are comparable to yours. You should also be aware of the existing competition in the area. What other buildings similar to yours are available, and how long have they been on the market? Have any of them sold or been leased? How long did they take to sell or lease? Your broker should be able to provide these answers almost immediately if they are familiar with the area. If you don't have a good gut feeling that your broker is representing your best interests or spending the proper amount of time on your property, it might be time for you to change that proverbial horse in the middle of the stream and hire a new broker.

If you follow my instructions in an earlier question on what you should be looking for in a broker, there will be less of a chance of this happening. However, if it does, contact one of the other brokers you interviewed, or interview one or two new brokers. Have them compare their marketing programs with the one you wish to replace.

Question: Do I have to give a new tenant free rent to help lease my building?

Answer: That depends. Is the market hot (high tenant demand), or is the market soft (low tenant demand)?

If it's a "landlords' market," meaning it's a hot market with very little vacancy in the marketplace and high prices, where tenants are having a hard time locating facilities, then no, you don't have to offer free rent. Free rent is commonly used as an incentive to get tenants to lease your building. I have seen many different types of markets, and when demand is low, there have been times when a tenant would receive a month of free rent for every year the property was leased (five months of free rent for a five-year lease). I have also seen markets where the tenant wouldn't receive any free rent because there were more tenants looking for space than was available.

The amount of free rent given to a tenant is determined by the current market conditions. Your local commercial real estate broker should know if free rent is warranted as an incentive to entice a tenant to lease your building.

Question: I have seen open houses for residential homes, but do they hold open houses for commercial property?

Answer: Yes. Much like residential open houses, sometimes a commercial broker will hold an open house for a commercial property.

In an effort to create more activity on a listing, sometimes the listing broker holds an open house, usually with some financial help from the owner of the property. An open house can be a small, quick get-together or a large extravaganza; it depends on the property and what kind of impression a broker and owner want to convey to the attendees.

Where residential open houses invite the public, a commercial open house is held for the cooperating commercial real estate brokers and not the public. A notice is sent to cooperating brokerage houses announcing details of the open house, including what type of food will be provided and what type of raffle or prize giveaway will be held to enhance attendance.

I once gave an open house at a cold storage facility. Inside a working 10,000-square-foot freezer (at zero degrees Fahrenheit), I had set up a table for vodka tasting. Not expensive but memorable.

If you want a well-attended open house, you need food and some type of raffle. The purpose of the raffle is to collect everyone's business card for marketing purposes. Sometimes there's a raffle for hundreds of dollars in cash, a big-screen TV, or even a vacation trip, and sometimes simple or gourmet food is served.

As soon as the raffle is held, the place clears out fast, so you must grab the brokers' attention quickly. Hand out brochures about the property being sold or leased so the brokers have something to take back to the office with them.

True Story

I can remember many memorable open houses over the course of my career. I attended one in the evening where they served lobster on fine china. I have had my photo taken with NFL Los Angeles Rams players and cheerleaders. I have been at open houses that offered elephant rides, camel rides, and helicopter rides. The more memorable an open house, the more memorable the property will be to the attendees.

I once attended an open house that had a contest for a Rolex watch. It was based on some sort of quiz show, but the questions were about the building that was the subject of the open house. All the brokers were split into two large groups and asked questions. Raising your hand for the correct answer would allow you to pass through to the next round. Once the group was down to about ten brokers, the questions were more detailed, and if you answered incorrectly, you left the group and sat down.

After the first round of questions, five agents remained, including me. The questions got harder. Now, just three of us remained. After another round of questions, only two of us remained. The questions kept coming, and when my competitor or I answered correctly, a loud cheer would rise up from the one hundred or so brokers watching with great anticipation. After five or six rounds of questions, it became clear that neither of us was going to answer incorrectly. So, instead of continuing with the questions, the host broker decided that the winner of the Rolex watch would be chosen by how many push-ups we could complete in one minute.

Of all exercises, push-ups were my least favorite. Great, I was about to embarrass myself in front of almost one hundred of my colleagues. Everything came down to this one minute. We got into place, someone said "go," and we both began doing push-ups in earnest. I never liked doing them in gym class, and trying to do them in a suit and tie on a cold concrete floor in the middle of an industrial building only made it harder. My biggest concern was looking weak and embarrassing myself in front of so many of my fellow brokers, but I pushed on.

True Story continues . . .

True Story continued . . .

> I felt like I was completing one push-up every second, and I didn't seem to tire. I never looked up. I just kept thinking, "I can do *anything* for one minute."
>
> At the end of one minute, they announced the winner: my competitor twenty-five, me forty-four. I had just won a Rolex watch! But more important to me, I wasn't publicly embarrassed.

Question: Should I give the tenant an option to renew the lease for an additional term or an option to purchase the property?

Answer: If you are leasing to a tenant, and the tenant has asked for an option to renew the lease for an additional term, this could be a good thing or a not-so-good thing, depending on a number of factors.

If you want to hold on to the property for a long time and don't have any interest in ever selling it, then giving the tenant an option to renew the lease for an additional term can make sense. However, it's important that you maintain the property's value by having the lease payments reflect the marketplace at the time.

So, when the tenant is given an option to renew, make sure there is a predetermination that the lease rate will increase on an annual basis and never go below the previous year's lease rate. When preparing options in leases, I prefer to have the determination of the lease rate based upon an annual percentage increase or current market rates at the time the option is exercised, whichever is higher. This way, you will keep pace with inflation.

If you don't want to give your tenant an option to renew the lease because you're unsure of your plans for the property, you could give your tenant the first right of refusal to lease the property. That way, if you decide to lease the property, they have the first right to lease it. One reason you might decide to put the property on the market is to see if you can get a much higher lease rate. If you receive an offer, you will be obligated to alert your existing tenant to see if they can match the offer.

Even if the lease doesn't contain an option to renew, as many tenants and owners communicate and interact with each other during the lease period, they can determine whether they want to continue their business relationship as tenant and landlord.

Question: Should you give your tenant an option to purchase the property?

Answer: My quick answer is no. If you give the tenant the option to purchase the property, you are always tied to the tenant. The tenant may have an option to purchase the property at a price below what the future market might be when the tenant exercises the option to purchase.

For example, suppose a tenant enters into a lease with an option to purchase a property for $150 per square foot. But after three years, the market for the property is at $225 per square foot. You have lost out on $75 per square foot.

A much more protective way to do this would be to give the tenant an option to purchase the property but have the purchase price increase on an annual basis by an amount of your choosing. Ultimately, the best choice would be to have the purchase price determined at the time the option is exercised. This rate would be at or near the actual market rate.

To keep yourself out of all those minutiae, you might offer your tenant a right of first refusal. That way, if you do put the property on the market for sale, you will contact them first to see if they wish to buy it. Of course, the purchase price in this case would be at the market rate.

The easiest and best thing to do is to not give an option to purchase at all. When you decide to sell the property, you can always ask your tenant first to see if they are interested. If not, you can put it on the market. However, I have found that it's best to put the property up for sale at the same time that you offer it to the tenant. That way, you have a tenant who is very motivated to purchase a property at the market rate and not necessarily at a discount because of your relationship with them.

Question: Should I be concerned about the type of tenant who wants to lease my property?

Answer: Yes.

If you own commercial property, especially an industrial property, there is a high probability that you could end up leasing it for many different types of use. Some of these uses come equipped with their own barrel of chemicals, grease, oil, or hazardous waste of your choosing.

This doesn't mean you shouldn't lease to these types of users. However, it does mean that you should closely observe the way the tenant operates their business and the way it impacts your property and the surrounding properties.

Let's say a chemical company wants to lease your property. What was their track record in previous facilities they operated in? Was the fire department called to their previous facility for chemical spills, fires, or any other reason? Do they operate their business in full compliance with all government agencies that have jurisdiction over what they do? Do they have to modify the building in order to contain a particular type of machine or storage area for chemicals or hazardous materials? As long as you know the answers to these and other questions that directly affect your property, and you have a written guarantee from the tenant that they will participate in any type of cleanup or remediation if something goes wrong, then you might feel more comfortable leasing to that tenant. If you don't want to handle such a monumental undertaking, you might want to limit the leasing of the property to a cleaner type of industrial use, such as warehousing, distribution, assembly, or another type of industrial use that doesn't use hazardous chemicals and/or materials.

True Story

One of the tasks that real estate brokers do a lot is show buildings to possible tenants. One day, I arrived at a building showing about half an hour before the tenant was to arrive for the tour. I wanted to turn the lights on and get the building ready for an easy, uninterrupted tour. This particular building was a 50,000-square-foot biomedical laboratory mostly comprising small, intricate offices with numerous chemical labs. It took almost five minutes to walk from the front of the building to the back of the building because there were so many hallways and corridors with twists and turns like a maze.

The owner of the building told me that there was an alarm pad in one of the offices not far from the entrance that I had to disarm by punching in the correct code. As soon as I opened the door, I could hear a continuous beep, beep, beep as I searched for the alarm pad. But I couldn't find the alarm pad quickly enough, and before I knew it, the most obnoxious, shrieking alarm blasted the air, piercing my ears and those of anyone in the vicinity. In less than three minutes, two of Garden Grove's finest pulled up to see what was going on. I showed the police my business card and told them what I was doing at the property. They checked things out, seemed satisfied, and left.

About fifteen minutes later, when I was closing the door to lock it, I punched the code on the keypad to set the alarm and must have gotten the numbers wrong because the alarm shrieked again. Within five minutes, the same two police officers returned to the building and told me I should learn to use the alarm pad. I readily agreed and apologized.

After a few more minutes, I composed myself and faced the awful, blinking alarm keypad that I still hadn't mastered. Once again, I double-checked the alarm code I had written down, knowing that after I entered it, I had thirty seconds to exit the building and close and lock the door. I thought I had it down, so I punched in the code, pressed the alarm button, and made my way to the exit.

Somehow, I made a wrong turn and wasted some of those precious thirty seconds. I made it to the door and dashed outside to lock up, but just as

True Story continues . . .

True Story continued . . .

I was turning the key, that terrible, ear-piercing alarm shot through the neighborhood once again. As I stood outside, the same two Garden Grove police officers drove by with their windows down, waving to me, obviously enjoying their day far more than I was. I think I even saw one of them laughing.

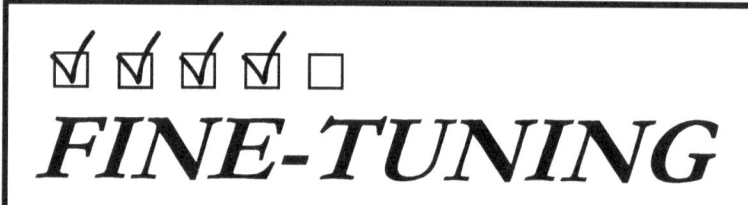

Question: Can I ask the tenant for more than one month's security deposit?

Answer: Yes. It's your property. You can ask for anything you want. That's the quick answer; however, there may be a more diplomatic way to obtain a larger security deposit if needed—and in forms other than money.

It seems like the more money a person has, the more banks and lenders want to lend them money. On the flip side, the less financially well-off you are—therefore more in need of a loan—the less banks and lenders want to lend you a dime.

It's the same way with a real estate security deposit. If a well-known, financially fit tenant wants to lease your property, you probably wouldn't ask them for more than a "normal" security deposit simply because you know they have the finances to pay the monthly rent. On the other hand, if an unknown, not-so-financially fit tenant wants to lease your property, you would probably want to have some added assurance that the monthly rent will be a regular monthly occurrence. So, you might want to demand a higher security deposit.

A security deposit isn't merely a means of ensuring payment of the monthly rent. A security deposit enables you to have funds readily available to repair any damage to the property or building caused by the tenant that is beyond the normal "wear and tear" provided for in the lease.

Also, don't have the security deposit noted in the lease as being the last month's rent. If the last month's rent is paid for with the security deposit, it will be very difficult to obtain additional money from the tenant for any repairs if you discover the building was damaged after they move out.

Always have your tenant pay the last month's rent, and then hold on to the security deposit until all damage beyond the normal wear and tear of a tenancy is itemized and repaired.

Now, getting back to how much of a security deposit you should request: if you feel the tenant is financially weak, maybe you shouldn't lease to the tenant in the first place. However, if you have interviewed the tenant, have seen the tenant's financials, and are leaning toward leasing to them but are still not 100% convinced, a higher security deposit might ease your mind. You can ask for two months, three months, or more. You might ask for prepaid rent. You can also have the tenant sign a personal guarantee, meaning that if the tenant defaults on a rent payment, you can go after the tenant's personal financial assets. I don't recall many landlords having to resort to this, but just knowing that a personal guarantee is hanging over their head is motivation enough for a tenant not to miss a rent payment.

Question: What is a TI allowance? Do I have to give a TI allowance to a tenant? What about incentives or free rent?

Answer: TI allowance stands for "tenant improvement allowance," sometimes known as TIA. Simply put, as an owner or landlord of a property, you may offer the tenant an allowance of money, building improvements, free rent, or any other item of value as an incentive for them to lease your building.

This is something that many developers who construct a new building have built into their leasing formula. A developer doesn't want to build a specific type of office that might exclude a tenant who doesn't wish for the configuration the developer has chosen. Instead, many owners will give a tenant a monetary TI allowance. The tenant can then use it for office space or any other type of improvement as long as it isn't too exotic and can be used by future tenants.

Some tenants will want a different office space configuration, additional electrical power installed, an additional loading door installed, etc. So, the tenant may ask for a TI allowance of a certain amount to cover those costs. You don't have to agree to a TI allowance. However, if the tenant is financially fit and appears to be the type of tenant you would want to lease your facility long-term, it would probably be wise to offer them some sort of allowance.

Depending on the state of the market, you can also offer a tenant an incentive to encourage them to move into your building more quickly or take a longer lease term. For example, if a tenant wants a three-year lease and you would like them to take a five-year lease, you could offer two months' free rent if they sign for five years. Or maybe you could reduce the fourth- and fifth-year lease rate increase if they agree to a five-year lease.

Whether it's a reduction in lease rate, free rent, or some other incentive, it makes sense to avail yourself of this option, if necessary.

Question: How can I receive more rent year after year? How is the rent increased?

Answer: It's always a good idea to have your rent increase on an annual basis. You want to keep the rent at least on pace with the rate of inflation. Your commercial building is an investment, so it makes sense for an investment to increase in value and income over time. One of the best ways to increase the rent is to have predetermined annual increases of a certain percentage or a certain dollar amount.

One way to calculate a monthly rent increase is to base it on the local consumer price index (or CPI). But it can be difficult to easily calculate a percentage change using the CPI, as there are various local CPIs and different ways to calculate them, which can lead to confusion.

To cover all your bases, establish the annual increase with a minimum CPI of 4% and a maximum of 7%. That way, if the CPI goes up by 3%, you will still get

4%, keeping you ahead of the inflation curve. Leases nowadays are moving away from using the CPI and going straight to an agreed-upon annual increase in rent.

Question: The tenant wants to remove the monument sign in the parking lot to create more parking. I told them it's okay if they are paying for it themselves. What do you think?

Answer: Under no circumstances should a monument sign be removed from your property unless you have permission from the city to do so or know you will be able to reinstall a monument sign of at least that size again. The reason is that city planners prefer monument signs to be located on the building itself so the street doesn't look too "junky."

In an effort to streamline the look of streets and avenues, many cities have language in their building codes stating that if a monument sign or pole sign is removed, it cannot be replaced or rebuilt. This could hurt signage and marketing, especially if the property is a retail establishment that relies on catching consumers' eyes with a street sign.

Question: My building has been available for lease for more than sixty days. What's going on? Why hasn't it leased?

Answer: If you were in constant communication with your commercial real estate broker, you would know exactly what was going on, and you would have been able to tell after the first thirty or forty days whether or not you should adjust your marketing program. Before you even list your property, you should know which transactions have taken place, for how much, which buildings are competing with yours, and the going lease rates.

If any comparable competitive buildings have been leased, you need to know why they were leased before yours. Who leased them and for how much? Why didn't you get the deal? If you can answer all these questions and know what's going on in the marketplace, then you shouldn't feel uneasy about your building being available. If, on the other hand, you don't know the answers to any of these questions, then you need to have a good discussion with your commercial real estate broker to find out why this is happening. You should never be left in the dark.

"I don't wish to be disturbed. If anyone calls, tell them I'm in the details."

Question: What are the best ways to research a possible tenant and check their true financial condition?

Answer: This is one of the valuable services a commercial real estate broker can provide.

Here are some of the financial documents you should obtain from a prospective tenant:

- tax returns for the previous few years

- balance sheets

- income statements

It's best to obtain these financial documents from the tenant's CPA. That way, you will obtain audited financial documents instead of unaudited ones.

Your commercial real estate broker probably also has access to various computer applications that can research a company's financial statements and company information. This can be very useful when trying to determine if someone is a viable tenant.

Besides obtaining financial documents, one of the best ways to find out more about a prospective tenant is to meet with them personally and walk through their existing facility. You will observe firsthand how they operate their business and be able to determine if this is something you want in your facility. A personal visit will also alert you to any red flags that might make you hesitate to lease to them (e.g., oil on the floor, unsafe working conditions, etc.).

Also, don't discount the opportunity to talk to their existing landlord. Ask about their payment history over the term of their lease, how cooperative they have been to their current landlord and neighbors during their occupancy, and the present landlord's opinion of the tenant.

Question: My current tenant's lease is expiring, and they want to extend the lease and add an option. This seems pretty easy, since most of it is already done. Can I do this without a real estate agent?

Answer: Whether you entered into that lease ten years ago or just two years ago, the commercial real estate marketplace has changed in that time. You need to have the most up-to-date information so you don't leave any money on the table when calculating the new lease rate.

For example, if you have a 10,000-square-foot building and you end up with just $0.03 less than what you could have renegotiated the lease for, you could be missing out on almost $11,000 over a three-year term.

Also, some tenants might ask for improvements if they are to continue leasing the space from you; this would most likely happen in a tenant's market. This is all negotiable, but as a landlord, you have some leverage because the tenant is already in your space, and moving to a new location can be very expensive.

Here's a good example: a do-it-yourself building owner called me up and wanted to renew the existing lease he had with his tenant. He thought a 3% increase was warranted, and I agreed, as a 3% annual increase was normal for the marketplace at that time. I asked him what rate he was currently receiving from his tenant. He told me he thought he was a little under market but was unaware of what the market rate was.

After a few questions, I discovered that the lease rate he was charging his tenant was, on average, $0.33 per square foot below the marketplace. The building was only 6,000 square feet, but charging his tenant $0.33 per square foot less than the market rate was depriving him of almost $2,000 per month! This was a man who had retired and was collecting aluminum cans in his garage.

I made sure he understood the status of the marketplace and the value of obtaining a market rate from his existing tenant and assisted him in completing a successful extension to his existing lease at a market rate that was acceptable to his tenant. The moral of the story: be aware of your marketplace and seek advice from a professional commercial real estate agent. It literally pays . . . in this case, $24,000 per year.

Question: Do I need an attorney to help write the lease?

Answer: That depends. More than 95% of all leases are standardized, have been around for years, and get updated as needed. These standardized leases are the result of the collaboration of many experienced attorneys. Why pay one attorney when many others have already done the work for you?

If the situation is more complex, such as a complicated option, a right of first refusal, or circumstances that are confusing even with the help of your commercial real estate broker, then I would recommend a real estate attorney.

In most cases, your real estate broker will be able to prepare the lease and all the appropriate items contained within the lease. You should be able to read the lease and understand it and have your commercial real estate agent explain anything that is unclear.

If, after an explanation from your real estate agent, you still don't understand what's contained in the lease, or you merely want to confirm what's in the lease, then this would be a good time to hire a real estate attorney for a few hours.

In the unlikely event that a tenant requests a particular type of lease specific to their business or an addendum that goes beyond the norm, or if you have a special circumstance that needs to be addressed, then this might also merit hiring a real estate attorney.

Question: The lease has been fully executed. When do I give the key to my new tenant? Is there a wrong time?

Answer: Just because you have a signed lease, the check for the first month's rent, and a security deposit doesn't mean you should hand over the key and give the tenant access to the property. Only accept a cashier's check, or, failing that, at least make sure the tenant's check can be cashed and deposited into your account . . . and make sure it clears!

Also, just as important, make certain the tenant has obtained liability insurance as is required in the signed lease. Confirm that you have been included in the liability insurance policy as an additional insured. This will help protect you if there's an accident on the property and someone wants to file a suit against you.

Once you have that information and are satisfied, you can release the key to your new tenant.

Question: Do I need a real estate broker to renew the lease I have with an existing tenant?

Answer: For essentially the same reasons you would hire a commercial real estate broker to lease your facility, you should hire a broker to renew the lease with your existing tenant.

If your tenant's lease is expiring soon, then the transaction probably occurred three years ago—maybe even five years ago or longer. During that time, market conditions have more than likely changed, along with the various rules, regulations, and laws impacting the tenant or the tenant's use. Using a professional commercial real estate broker to help renew your lease ensures that you have the most up-to-date documentation, the best terms for your circumstances, and the highest lease rate possible.

For example, a commercial building owner called me asking for the status of lease rates in the neighborhood in which he owned his building. He had been leasing to the existing tenant for more than eight years, but the lease rate he was charging them was well below the current market rate. He didn't know how to go about telling his tenant he wanted to increase the rent to bring it up to the market rate.

I told him we could probably increase the rent—not to the full market rate, but it would be a more substantial increase than he would have asked for. The new rate would also be enough below market for the tenant to continue to feel they were receiving a fair deal and be encouraged not to move out. Once we renewed the lease, the owner was receiving $0.27 per square foot more, and the tenant was still $0.05 to $0.06 below the market rate. This was truly a win-win for both parties.

True Story (I wish it wasn't)

Question (actually, more like a statement): My existing tenant wanted an option to renew the existing lease on my building for an additional period of time. I had a friend of mine negotiate and prepare this option for me. My friend has leased some properties in the past, so I'm pretty confident he knew what he was doing.

The deal is now completed, and the best part is that I didn't have to pay a commission to a commercial real estate broker to do something so easy. Sounds great, right?

Answer: Here's what happened. The owner's (lessor's) friend put together a two-page addendum extending the original lease between the lessor and the lessee for five years and also gave the lessee two additional five-year options to renew the lease. The rate of increase of the lease per year was fixed at 2.25%, which sounds okay until you look back at the renewal lease rate and realize that the first-year lease rate of the option term was 35% below the current market rate.

The market rate was $1.00 per square foot, but the renewal was at $0.65 per square foot, which was $0.35 per square foot below the current market. At this rate, it would take eleven years for the lease rate to increase to the current market rate . . . eleven years!

Multiplying $0.35 per square foot by the square footage of approximately 27,000 equals $9,450 per month. Multiply this by five years (120 months), and it totals $1,134,000.

The owner will lose $9,450 per month and a total of $1,134,000 during the first five years of the option period and will never be able to recapture it. This doesn't even take into account the two additional five-year options.

Yes, the lessor did save the $45,000 in commission a commercial real estate broker with market knowledge might have charged to negotiate and prepare an addendum. But the lessor had to forgo $1,134,000 to do so. *Ouch!*

There is a moral here, and by now, you recognize it.

CHAPTER **4** FOUR

"In real estate, you make 10% of your money because
you're a genius and 90% because you catch a great wave."

— Jeff Greene

I Am a User Who Wants to

Lease a Property

You are what America calls an entrepreneur, the type of person whose ideas and drive cannot be stopped. It started off with an idea, then moved to your garage, and then public storage. Now, you think you may have graduated to needing a "more official place." It may be time to lease a commercial building for your business.

Maybe you're an existing tenant and have been leasing space for a long time, but now you need more space to do what you do more effectively. No problem. You can find a new space yourself. That is how you have always done things in the past.

Wait a minute . . . you don't want to do something that will interrupt your business or take your attention away from running the day-to-day operation. If you are going to make a commitment for a year, three years, or maybe even five years, you should get some help from someone who knows everything there is to know about leasing commercial space. Someone who will be on your side.

Don't think of it as handing over the entire process to a commercial real estate broker. Think of it as having a partner on your team for this new level of operation.

Oh, and one more thing: all this help won't cost you a penny! It's free! Read on.

STARTING OUT

Question: Do I need a broker to help me find a space?

Answer: No, you don't need a broker, but it's a good idea if you want to save time and money.

Anyone can search for commercial space if they can afford to take time away from their business. A commercial real estate broker, however, does a lot more than just research and locate a commercial space. They use their expertise in the leasing process.

A broker starts with a good understanding of your business and gives you advice as to the space best suited to your business. The broker then uses inside resources and inside information to locate the best available space that offers you not only the best situation for your particular business but also the best deal. Furthermore, a commercial real estate broker can be by your side from the time your search begins until the lease is signed and beyond.

Question: I'm thinking about moving my business and leasing a new space. Where do I start?

Answer: The first thing to do is decide whether moving into a new space is the right choice.

You can do this by asking yourself the following questions:

- Do I want to look for a space on my own or hire a commercial broker to assist me?

- Is it a good time to move?

- How important is location?

- How much space do I need?

- How much can I afford?

- How long will it take to find a new space?

- How will the new space benefit the company and its future?

- What does it cost to move?

- What else is involved in moving? Furniture, phones, computers, copy/fax/postage machines, internet access, etc.?

- Can I afford to lose business or employees during the transition?

- How long does the entire process take from the beginning of the search until move-in day?

The above are just some of the many questions that you will want to have the answers to before you begin the process. It's very important to interview commercial real estate brokers who can help you answer these questions and give you an idea as to the type of facilities available for your type of business.

Quick Thought: *More than likely, you will encounter a commercial real estate broker while searching for a space. The broker will be representing the owner of a property you may have called about. Who do you think the broker represents? The property owner, of course. You need your own representation.*

Question: Why do I need a broker?

Answer: Sellers and landlords almost always use a broker to represent them in sale or lease negotiations. Buyers and tenants should do the same so they can stay focused on their company.

When a professional commercial real estate broker assists a tenant in leasing a property, the tenant saves an average of 15% on the lease compared to those who negotiate for themselves. This is especially true upon renewal of an existing lease. Tenants will also often receive other benefits such as construction allowances and more lease flexibility.

The broker's fee is usually paid by the seller or landlord, so don't think that you can't afford a commercial real estate broker.

Question: Is finding a space without hiring a broker a good idea?

Answer: The answer is no. You, as a tenant, don't enter into a lease very often, but a commercial real estate broker deals with leasing negotiations daily. Think of it this way. Would you go to the IRS for an audit without taking your CPA to represent you? Would you go on a jungle safari without a guide? Again, the answer is no.

Question: What kind of loading space do I need?

Answer: Do you need to be able to drive trucks or other vehicles into the warehouse? If so, then you need grade-level loading. Will you have products delivered or picked up by eighteen-wheeler or UPS-type trucks? If the answer is an eighteen-wheeler, you might need dock-high loading and a truck staging area big enough for eighteen-wheelers to maneuver. Not all trucks and dock-high doors are the same height. So, check to see if the dock-high doors have load levelers. These are almost a must-have if you plan on receiving trucks. Whatever the case, make sure the industrial property has what you need, and if not, ask if the landlord is willing to install what you need.

Trailers and trucks used to be forty-five feet long, but they can be up to sixty feet long these days, which means you may need at least a 120-foot turning area. Older industrial properties may not be able to accommodate this. So, before signing a lease, do a test run with the type of truck that will be servicing your facility to ensure they can maneuver around the property without difficulty.

Question: I've got plenty of time because my lease doesn't expire for another nine months. That's enough time, right?

Answer: Maybe, maybe not.

This could be contingent on the type of business you have and the process required to move it. I have worked with warehouse and distribution companies that can literally move in a weekend. I have also worked with companies that have an elaborate manufacturing or assembly facility that takes much longer to move because of the type of equipment and electrical distribution to the equipment. Finally, I have worked with companies that needed a specific license to operate in a particular area, and sometimes it would take three to six months to obtain it.

It's important to carefully study every nuance of your move to make sure that you have enough time to accomplish it. This is why a commercial real estate broker can be very a valuable tool in your decision-making process. Chances are the broker, or a colleague who has worked with a similar type of operation, can impart that knowledge and those lessons to you for your benefit.

Question: How far in advance should I start planning a renewal or a move?

Answer: That depends on the size of the space needed and how specialized the use is.

A tenant should start working with a broker anywhere from six months to a year prior to the expiration of the lease or before the new space is needed. This allows plenty of time to understand the future of the company, determine the role real estate should play in the future, search the market for all options, negotiate the terms of the deal, and document that deal in a lease.

A good broker will stay involved with the tenant over the term of the lease. They will help the tenant review landlord correspondence and operating expense bills throughout the lease term to ensure the tenant doesn't pay more than they should.

True Story

Very early in my career, I had a client looking for a large facility for his company. About once a week, I would pick up a well-dressed older gentleman I'll call Jack to tour large industrial buildings in many different areas of Orange County. We would walk through a 50,000-square-foot building, then an 80,000-sqare-foot building, and as we would walk through the building, he would tell me of the grand plans for his business and the many people ready to occupy the new facility as soon as he chose the appropriate location. He spoke of investors who couldn't wait to invest millions in the business and thought that, after a few years, they would be needing many more facilities.

Week after week I picked up Jack, who was always anxious to see the next building. No matter which facility I showed him, there was always something just not right about it. After many weeks and many tours, it hit me that Jack didn't want to lease a facility. Jack wanted to put a tie on and walk through large facilities as a VIP so he could feel important. Finally, I told Jack that if he saw a facility he thought would work for his company, he should call me, and I would help him.

Over the next few months, I was certain I would read about a large transaction being completed by Jack and another broker, or I would see Jack's sign on a large building, but I never did. And I never heard from Jack again.

Question: Can I use the real estate agent who sold me my house to negotiate my lease or help me purchase a building?

Answer: You could use the plumber who came to fix your drain to help you with your electrical wiring, but it probably isn't the best of ideas. Given the unique issues that arise with commercial real estate, it probably isn't a good idea. Real estate is highly specialized today, much like other industries. You should use a commercial real estate broker who is best able to accomplish your goals.

You are about to make a decision that you will have to live with for possibly many years. Get the best representation you can.

When buying a house to live in, use a residential agent. When buying or leasing a commercial property, use a commercial real estate broker. Even though I have been a commercial real estate broker for more than thirty-five years, I would not list a residential property, including my own. I would rather pay a small commission to make sure it is listed properly and legally, with a broker who has the best knowledge and experience in a particular neighborhood.

Quick Thought: *The information regarding available commercial properties on the Internet can often be very dated. Listings that have already sold and leased may remain online for months . . . or longer.*

Question: Can I search for my own lease or building purchase?

Answer: Yes, absolutely. But why would you?

If a property is listed with a commercial real estate broker, the commissions are built into the price and rent. So, you don't save any money by not using a broker to represent you. You are also taking valuable time away from your business.

Most businesspeople are experts in their businesses but probably not in real estate. So, remaining focused on their business while having a no-cost commercial real estate expert handle the real estate seems a much better solution.

Question: What are the pros and cons of using a commercial real estate broker?

Answer: Everyone wants to save a buck, and if hard work and perseverance can knock a few thousand off the cost of a real estate deal, many of us are inclined to go forward alone. But is it worth it to sift through scores of listings in the target area and engage in negotiations without employing a commercial real estate broker? The following will examine the pros and cons of finding your own commercial real estate space versus using a broker's expertise.

Potential cost savings

Unwillingness to pay a broker's commission is one of the top reasons why companies choose to forgo using an agent. However, businesses seldom have to pay out of pocket for the commission. The landlord has already planned to pay a 6% commission to the listing broker. The commission is usually divided between the brokers equally (50%–50%) but can be as lopsided as 90%–10% in favor of the listing agent.

In general, using a broker to help you locate and negotiate a deal will cost you nothing. The cost savings on a purchase or lease are almost always achieved by benefiting from the broker's market knowledge, as well as their skill, their access to privileged information, and their experience in negotiations. A business owner could successfully navigate the process but might miss out on important market information that a broker would probably already have simply by virtue of working in the marketplace on a daily basis.

Who is watching your back?

Listing agents are duty-bound to protect the landlord's interest. So, if a company searching for real estate only works with listing agents, they must rely on their own judgment and expertise to protect the company's interests. This creates a decided disadvantage at the negotiation table, as the landlord is the only party represented by professionals familiar with the process.

An agent who represents the tenant will prioritize your company's interests at every stage of the process. They can search for properties listed with many brokerages while taking your company's situation and needs into account. This greatly reduces the chaos of the real estate market for you and enables the agent to single out the properties that best fit your needs.

Working only with listing agents might also limit the properties you are shown. They might be motivated to steer you to their own listed properties in order to receive the maximum commission.

The value of time

Without a broker, sifting through the list of available properties and determining their suitability for your business might seem overwhelming. A broker brings experience and a solid understanding of the markets in your metropolitan area to the table and can help find the best location for you.

In addition to alleviating the significant investment of time needed to find a property, a broker can save you time as the deal progresses by making offers, organizing inspections, negotiating and renegotiating terms, and completing reams of paperwork. Because a broker has the experience and connections required to search for a property and complete all the contingent steps toward signing the lease, the overall process can be drastically streamlined, which will save you time.

Commercial real estate market knowledge provides an edge

Commercial real estate brokers pride themselves on knowing the local market and can help companies find the most profitable spots for their specific type of business.

They also pay thousands of dollars for proprietary information and market data reports on sales and leasing, including traffic count demographics and comparable leases and sales. They often know if offers have been made on a property and why those offers did not translate into a transaction. Possessing insight and an excellent understanding of the marketplace is an extremely valuable asset, and a commercial real estate broker can obtain this edge for you.

Commercial real estate negotiation

Negotiations can be complex and stressful, so it's helpful to have an advocate on your side. A commercial real estate broker negotiates for a living and can provide a buffer between the sometimes-rocky process and the client.

Brokers can also sift through a lease and spot hidden charges or profit centers for the landlord. Leases are legal documents that no one likes to read; they are confusing and full of jargon that often obscures the meaning. A good broker can read and interpret these legal documents and help you navigate lease clauses that could be harmful to you or your business.

Question: How do you know if you should lease or purchase a building?

Answer: What are your company's long-term goals? What are *your* long-term goals? Do you see your company expanding multiple times in the future? What does it cost to lease versus purchase and own a facility? These are just a few of the questions you want to ask yourself.

One of the first things you should do is contact a commercial real estate broker and have the broker compare purchasing a facility to leasing the same type of facility. This is called a "lease vs. buy analysis." Once this analysis has been completed and your broker has discussed and explained it to you, you might take your analysis to a CPA to discuss all of the tax advantages and disadvantages of both options.

When considering leasing or purchasing a facility, it's best to thoroughly evaluate where your company is headed and what expansion plans you have for your company. If the results of the analysis are fairly close, I would try to convince you to purchase a facility.

A business owner will often sell their business or shut their business down after successfully running it for years. If the business owner owns the facility, they will have a wonderful retirement fund in the form of a commercial building that generates monthly income. Whatever the case, do a good bit of analysis with a commercial real estate broker and follow up with a CPA.

Question: I'm in the market for a food preparation/storage building. It doesn't seem like there are many out there. What do I do?

Answer: Whether it's a food service building or any other specific type of industry, the best possible course of action is to employ a real estate broker specializing in that specific type of use. Almost every real estate agent who has been in the business for multiple years knows how to find a food preparation building, but far fewer of those agents know about the intricacies of refrigeration/freezers/food prep rooms/FDA approval, etc.

This is why it's important to seek out a broker who only deals in a specific category of use. There are brokers who specialize in food buildings, church buildings, auto-related buildings, and many other specific categories. Be sure to arm yourself with an agent who knows exactly what you are looking for. The process will go much more smoothly.

Bob didn't know which door to choose...the
ground level door or the overhead door.

Question: What is the difference between a ground-level door and an overhead door?

Answer: Tomayto/tomahto . . . potayto/potahto. Better read on . . .

A ground-level door and an overhead door are the same thing. It is sometimes called an overhead door because when it is open, it is over your head, not off to the side of the opening as if it were a rolling door.

There is, however, a difference between a ground-level door and a dock-high door (or a truck well door). The difference here is pretty self-explanatory. Where people sometimes get hung up is in differentiating between dock-high loading doors and truck well loading doors. The difference is not in the way the door looks but in how the truck approaches the building for loading and unloading.

Dock-high loading doors are about four and a half feet above ground level. As a truck backs in to load and unload products, the bottom of the truck bed is aligned with the bottom opening of the dock's door. This is similar to a truck well loading area. However, instead of the loading door being four and a half feet above the ground, the door is at ground level, and there is a well or depression in front of the door that the truck backs into. It backs its way down the truck well until the bed of the truck and the bottom of the loading door area are level. These depressions or wells can be anywhere from twenty to forty feet long or longer. The longer the well, the less of an incline the truck is on, which helps keep the load in the truck as level as possible.

Many truckers and users prefer dock-high doors because they keep the truck perpendicular (level), whereas a truck well will put the truck bed at a slight angle, which can sometimes shift the load in a truck.

Question: What are amps? What are volts? Is 800 amps better than 400 amps? Why should I know about amps? And what do all those numbers on the front of the electrical meter box mean?

Answer: It's important that you know the basics of amps and volts and have a working knowledge of how electricity is utilized in your business. Beyond that, it's best to employ the services of a professional electrician.

All buildings are supplied with electrical service, and some buildings have a greater supply of electricity than others. Some distribution buildings are supplied with a minimal number of amps because they mainly require electricity for lighting and not to run machinery. Other buildings will be serviced with more electricity because the building might house a company that requires a considerable amount of machinery to manufacture a product.

Here's an easy one: an 800-amp electrical panel is more powerful than a 400-amp electrical panel. Generally, small buildings or multi-tenant units will have at least 100 amps of power. This is enough to run lights, small electrical hand tools, and a small office area. The larger the building, the greater the variety of tenants and types of use it can accommodate. Choosing to service a building with a higher amount of electricity allows a building owner to accommodate different types of businesses. The more amps, the more electricity, resulting in a better chance of accommodating users who have a need for more electricity.

Electrical power is a topic that comes up daily in the world of industrial real estate. Prospective tenants need to be certain that the power in a space will meet their electrical needs, while savvy building owners need to realize that bringing adequate power into their building is a long-term investment in their property.

In our industry, we regularly hear and use terms like three-phase, amps, and volts. But what does it all mean?

Amperage, Voltage, and Watts Explained

Amperage (amps): the amount of current flowing through a wire. For reference, this is similar to the amount of water flowing through a hose in a pressure washer.

Voltage (volts): the pressure that pushes amps through the circuit. This is similar to the power of the pump that pushes the water through the hose of that pressure washer.

Watts: the measurement of electricity used (amps × volts = watts). Watts are your energy consumption and are similar to how hard the water hits a surface when sprayed with the pressure washer.

If you're a little confused or maybe lost at this point, call a professional electrician. If you're still with me, hang on; I'm almost done.

Three-Phase Power vs. Single-Phase Power

Three-phase power is the industry standard in manufacturing, warehouse, and industrial buildings across the globe. You will only find single-phase power in your house or small, nonindustrial buildings—or in industrial buildings that were constructed more than forty years ago. Three-phase power allows for smaller, less expensive wiring and lower voltages, which makes it safer and far less expensive to run.

Single-phase power has only one current and one voltage output per cycle. This power current travels in waves. When the wave passes through zero, the power supplied (voltage) is zero.

Three-phase power has three currents and three voltage outputs per cycle. These three currents travel in waves that overlap each other so the level of power supplied remains consistent (less of a chance of a power outage or blown fuse).

If you got through that, you are to be commended; if not, there are electricians standing by to help you.

Question: I need 800 amps of electrical power. The electrical meter says, "800 amps." Am I good to go?

Answer: Stop. No, you're not good to go. Remember the old cliché, "Never judge a book by its cover"? Well, consider the electrical meter box a large metal book cover.

I have learned over the course of my years in the commercial real estate business that what appears to be so isn't necessarily so. Just because a metal plate with electrical power information engraved on it looks real (it more than likely is) doesn't mean that what it states is true. It might be completely wrong about the type of power being delivered to the building, into the power panel, and distributed to the various machinery, electrical equipment, and lights.

Modifications are often done to the electrical panels of an industrial building. Amps may have been added, removed, or rerouted. It happens all too often that a prospective tenant sees a 400-amp plate attached to an electrical panel and discovers later that the actual electrical service to the building is different. This can be a very costly error to resolve.

If your business is dependent on the amount and type of electrical power servicing a building and will be using more than basic electrical lighting, it's very important that you employ the services of a licensed electrical contractor or electrician to help verify the amperage entering the building. It might also be advisable to ask the local electric company any questions you might have regarding the electrical service to the property. A little investigative work on the front end can save a lot of time and a great deal of money on the back end.

The local electric company that services the area can often visit the building site to verify the electrical power at no charge.

Question: What is an HVAC, and why do I need to worry about it?

Answer: HVAC stands for "heating, ventilation, and air-conditioning." You need to worry about it when you are too hot, when you are too cold, or when it doesn't work.

Before you lease a property, be sure to have the HVAC unit inspected by a professional air-conditioning company and have their findings delivered to you in writing. If there is a problem, be sure you have the landlord take care of these issues before you take occupancy or before you sign the lease. Once all of that is settled, the typical lease states that it's the tenant's responsibility to have an HVAC service contract, which means you will have to have a professional air-conditioning or heating company come out and inspect the unit, possibly change some filters, and tweak or adjust any small items before they grow into large items.

Usually, the cost of such an HVAC service contract is minimal, somewhere between $200 and $400 per year.

When a building doesn't have an existing ductwork system to distribute conditioned air, it can be expensive and problematic to install a conventional central air-conditioning system. Some older buildings or smaller multi-tenant units don't have central air and heat and are equipped with a box air-conditioning unit. This isn't necessarily a bad thing, and it just might be a more economical way to supply a small office area with cool air and heat.

The worst time to find out that the air-conditioning doesn't work is during a heatwave in July. So, just because it's January or February and you're cold, don't let that stop you from testing the air-conditioning (and the heater) before you sign the lease.

Question: What is floor load, and why do I need to know about it?

Answer: Floor load is the load that a floor in a building may be expected to carry safely if uniformly distributed. It's usually calculated in pounds per square foot of area.

Let's say you have a heavy piece of machinery that weighs ten tons (20,000 lbs.). If that piece of machinery stamps out a product every day, several tons of additional weight and force will continuously pound, shake, and vibrate the concrete floor that the machine is placed upon. If the floor load is less than the weight of the machinery, or less than what is needed to support an active machine on a daily basis, the floor will crack or break, possibly altering the specs of the machine—or worse, ruining the machine and the concrete floor within the building.

It's always a good idea to consult a structural engineer if you are concerned about an existing floor or are thinking of placing a substantial piece of machinery or other heavy items on a floor in a commercial building.

Zoning Wars

Question: Property zoning has me confused. What are M1, M2, GM, C1, C2, etc.?

Answer: Different municipalities have different ways of coding and zoning their land. GM usually stands for "general industrial" (I know of a few cities that have reversed the letters to read "MG," which means the exact same thing). As an area allows for heavier industrial use, numbers will be added to the letter. For example: M1 is industrial use; M2, heavy industrial use; M3, heaviest industrial use.

A property zoned C is normally designated for commercial/retail use. Sometimes retail zones are designated with—of all things—an R, and office zones are mostly designated with an O. But it's best to consult the zoning department of whatever particular city you're interested in to find out which letters of the alphabet designate each particular zone.

Question: I have toured many industrial buildings, and some of them don't have a water heater. Why not? Is running hot water not a requirement?

Answer: While it's nice to have running hot water, in many cities, it's perfectly legal not to have a water heater. While government agencies might require a restroom, a restroom doesn't have to be equipped with hot water.

Needless to say, a smart landlord should install a water heater for rentability and the comfort of his tenants, but some just don't.

I'm starting this "Strategy" section off with a question that you might think belongs in the "Starting Out" section. However, if you have skipped to this section and are thinking of going it alone (without a broker), then read this next question and answer.

Question: I have leased commercial property for years and years. I know what I'm looking for, and I know what I can afford. Do I still need a real estate broker?

Answer: The quick answer would be yes . . . and the slow, thoughtful answer would also be yes.

A competent commercial real estate broker knows exactly what's going on in the neighborhood in which you are thinking of locating your business. And if they are worth their salt, they will know where the best facilities for your business might become available in the next few months. Wouldn't you hate to lease a property only to discover one month later that a much better facility that would have suited your business even better just became available? It's really important to have the background information that only a commercial real estate broker can provide.

Also, hiring a commercial real estate broker probably won't cost you a thing because, in most cases, they are paid for by the owner who has listed his building for lease. Any time you can obtain professional advice and get the best "inside information" possible, take it!

Question: What is a representation letter or exclusive agreement, and should I sign one?

Answer: The tenant's representative (broker) may present you with a representation letter to sign for your own protection. The letter protects you by stating that you are working with only one tenant representative. It also protects the tenant representative by ensuring that they will get paid if the lease is signed. The payment will likely be made by the landlord, not you, the tenant.

If a tenant representative doesn't have a letter signed by the prospective tenant, they will most likely only perform a simple property search or only mention availabilities that are their own listings. If you want to get the most out of a brokerage community, I would recommend you sign an exclusive agreement instead of working with several agents on a nonexclusive basis. You will get a much better return on your investment of time and energy.

Question: Now that I've hired a tenant representative, what should I expect from them?

Answer: You should expect your tenant representative to think solely of your interests and give you advice to achieve your ultimate goal of leasing an appropriate facility for yourself and your company.

The tenant representative helps you determine how much space you need, where to locate your business, and what amenities are most important. Then, they find the space that best fits your needs and negotiate for it. When it comes to the negotiation, make sure your tenant representative knows what is important to you.

Question: I see signs everywhere! There must be more property to see than what you're showing me!?!

Answer: I have personally answered this question numerous times.

Regarding signs: many multi-tenant building projects have an "available" sign on the building continuously, whether there is an availability or not. They do this to advertise or obtain more leads, or perhaps they may have a month-to-month tenant and can make a space available in thirty days. Sometimes a sign is left on a building for weeks or even months after it has been leased merely because the broker is trying to squeeze as much advertising as possible out of the sign.

It's in a commercial broker's best interests to show you *all* the property that is available because a broker works on commission and doesn't make an income until you sign a lease.

Some of the reasons a broker isn't showing an available building might be that the building isn't the size you are looking for, the building has been leased, the amount of office space is drastically different than what is needed, etc.

A tenant looking for space should be shown multiple properties, even when some of the items required are not present on a property. For example, if dock-high loading is needed and the building doesn't have it, a dock door can be constructed; if fire sprinklers are needed and the building doesn't have any, they can be installed, etc. It's more important that the location and the flow of the building work for the tenant's business.

Question: Can I get a better lease in a multi-tenant building or a freestanding building?

Answer: This depends on a number of items regardless of whether the property is freestanding or part of a multi-tenant park. These items include whether the owner has owned the property for twenty years or just recently purchased it. Here are a few scenarios to illustrate my point.

- If a landlord has recently purchased a property, they will probably need to lease it at a higher rate to cover the higher tax basis.

- A landlord of a multi-tenant park might be more likely to accommodate your lease offer if your lease constitutes a large portion of the property as opposed to a much smaller percentage of the property.

- A freestanding building with a long-time owner and a low tax base might present the perfect conditions to enable a tenant to obtain a lower lease rate. This makes the case yet again as to why it's crucial to have representation so you can learn about the property's backstory and the owner's reasons for leasing.

Question: Should I make more than one offer? Should I make multiple offers on multiple properties?

Answer: You want to be extremely careful if and when you decide to do something like this. If you make multiple offers and they are all accepted, then you could be liable for any offer that is accepted by the other party. You probably want to have the guidance of a commercial real estate broker to make an offer for you. If you do decide to make more than one offer at a time, then it's important to include language in your offer stating that "these are the general terms" on which you would be willing to lease a commercial property; however, the only legally binding agreement would be an actual mutually signed lease document.

This way, if you have two or three facilities that are all suitable for your type of business and time is of the essence, you could do this. It might be best if your commercial real estate broker mentions to the owner that you are submitting more than one offer at a time, which could have the benefit of creating some competition amongst the owners. One word of caution: do not submit multiple offers with multiple brokers. Use the same broker to represent you on all offers in order to coordinate offers, responses, etc.

Question: What information and documents do I need to give the owner of a property to review?

Answer: At the very least, you will have to complete a lease application with information about your company as well as personal information. That same lease application will likely include some sort of permission for the landlord to run a credit check on you. You may be asked for at least two years of financial statements, including income statements and balance sheets, and, most likely, you will need to hand over two years of tax returns for you and/or the company.

I have found over the years that landlords often place more importance on your existing operation and your previous or existing landlord's opinion of you than they do on financial documents. So, if your current location is operational (and as clean and orderly as possible), invite the landlord or the landlord's broker to tour your operation. I have seen this work in favor of the tenant almost every time. If those things check out, you will be well on your way.

Question: My agent submitted my offer to lease to the building owner's broker, but I haven't heard anything for days. What's going on, and what do I do now?

Answer: When your agent prepares your offer, make sure there is a date on your offer stating when your offer becomes void or voidable by you. This may be a catalyst for the owner to respond sooner. If, after the voidable date, you have not received a response, your agent needs to investigate.

Three or maybe four days without hearing a response is not uncommon. Unfortunately, the agent who represents you in your search for an appropriate commercial facility doesn't have complete control over the owner's broker, let alone the owner. There could be a number of reasons why an acceptance or response has not come back. The owner may be out of town; there may be other offers that the owner and his broker are working on; there may be an issue with the owner's broker. To guard against too many days passing before you receive a response, *have your agent contact the owner's broker for an explanation* so they can tell you when a response will be forthcoming.

Ask your agent if they have completed offers on similar types of buildings and any other questions that may be appropriate. Make sure your agent is transparent with you at all times. Most agents will be happy to answer all of your questions, and they will be very open with you. You don't want to find out that *your* agent is the one making things take longer than they should.

If you feel that a response to your offer is taking too much time—or worse, your offer is being ignored—think about moving on. There are other buildings out there.

Question: How do I negotiate the best lease deal possible?

Answer: If you are represented by an experienced commercial real estate broker in whom you have full faith and who dives headfirst into the process, you should be confident that you are obtaining the best information and, hence, the best deal, as the broker will have educated you about the marketplace. You can also collect data on those transactions that will give you a real-time understanding of the deals happening in the marketplace so you can compare them to your situation.

Also know this: it isn't a done deal just because you have been given a lease from the lessor to sign. The opportunity to negotiate isn't over. A lease between two parties isn't deemed completed until the lease has been signed by and delivered to both parties. Once you receive the lease to execute, make a list of all the provisions that you don't understand, don't agree with, or need clarified. You and your broker can respectfully present the prospective landlord with a list of these items. The landlord will most likely be receptive, respond positively, and be willing to modify the items and work with you.

Question: What is a conditional use permit, and do I need one?

Answer: A conditional use permit (sometimes known as a CUP) is a zoning exception granted by the city or county that allows the property owner to use his land in a way not otherwise permitted within the particular zoning district.

All property in a particular city is divided into zones. Each zone is designated with certain permitted, conditional, and prohibited uses of the land. The purpose of a conditional use permit is to allow for special consideration of certain specified uses that may or may not be compatible with an area depending on the specifics of the particular project. The conditional use permit process gives the city sufficient flexibility to determine whether a specific use on the given site will be compatible with the environment and the general plan of the city.

In reviewing a conditional use permit application, the staff and planning commission of the city will evaluate various items:

- building placement

- environmental concerns regarding the use

- traffic generation

- noise

- hours of operation

- adequacy of parking

- circulation

- proposed intensity

- landscaping

- overall compatibility with adjoining and surrounding properties

- other related development impacts

Conditions may be imposed on the property's use, as necessary, to ensure that the proposed use will be as compatible as possible with the surrounding properties and environment and not create undue pressure or hardship on surrounding businesses.

Question: What is the process for obtaining a conditional use permit?

Answer: Early on, the applicant should contact the city's planning staff to determine the general plan and zoning ordinance criteria for the site under consideration. It's important that the proposed use is as consistent as possible with the city's general plan and zoning ordinance. If, for some reason, the proposed business or operation is not allowed under the city's current zoning regulations, a conditional use permit may be applied for and obtained to enable that particular business to be located in that particular building.

Before spending a lot of money and time on the process of obtaining a conditional use permit (they can be very expensive), schedule a preliminary review meeting to discuss your eligibility and the feasibility of the request. This will allow city staff to review the request for compliance with the city's general plan, zoning ordinance, specific plans, and other applicable city standards.

City staff—this includes planning, building, public works, police, and the fire authority—will assess possible concerns including, but not limited to, infrastructure requirements, traffic, landscaping, building design, environmental impact, and safety criteria.

Once you have some positive feedback from the various city agencies and feel you would have a very good chance of obtaining the conditional use permit, you should then submit your formal application and all supporting materials that the city might need, along with the fee.

Once you have submitted your application to the city, it's sometimes reviewed and approved or denied by the planning commission quickly. But more often than not, it's discussed at a city council meeting. It's heard by the city council, and any surrounding businesses or property owners are invited to speak for or against the proposed CUP. It's then voted on. If all goes well and you have done your homework, you will be granted a conditional use permit to operate your business in that particular building.

Sometimes a CUP is approved with contingencies. Such contingencies could be the reconfiguration of parking spaces, additional landscaping, increased safety features added to the building, etc.

Conditional use permits are granted for a specific property only and cannot be transferred to any other property. Some conditional use permits can remain in effect in perpetuity; others might be for a specific time period. This will all depend on the city and county you are applying in.

Sometimes a conditional use permit can be revoked by the city if the city feels that the business is not operating as per the guidelines mandated when the CUP was approved. Each city or municipality has different rules and guidelines, and it's important to understand what those guidelines are before forging ahead with the conditional use permit application process. The entire process can take four to ten weeks depending on the complexity of the conditional use permit or the scheduled meeting times of the city's planning commission and city council.

With adequate explanation from city officials and guidance from your commercial real estate broker, you can usually get through the process without much difficulty. However, you might consider hiring someone who makes it their business to help guide an applicant through the CUP process if the business use is complex and the city is skeptical.

Question: If I'm going to lease a building for three years or more, can I get free rent?

Answer: Basically, when you ask the landlord for free rent, you are asking for an incentive to move into a commercial building.

Sometimes the landlord will offer these incentives willingly to attract new tenants to a building that is in need of occupants. However, when the market favors landlords—meaning there is a shortage of available space—these incentives dry up, and sometimes they are not offered at all.

Incentives can come in the form of free rent, a lower lease rate, smaller increases in the rent schedule, a build-out allowance, or some other way to soften the initial financial blow for the proposed tenant.

Obtaining free rent or any other type of incentive is really determined by how hot the market is and how motivated a landlord is to have you as a tenant.

Quick Thought: Know what your net cost is. I've seen this cost range from $0.07 per square foot to as much as $1.10 per square foot. So, be aware of all the expenses beyond base rent.

Question: How do you know when it is the right time to relocate?

Answer: Do you have to use a forklift to remove items or materials from your warehouse and place them in the yard just so you can get to the business at hand? Do you have trucks backing out from your driveway onto the street in order to load and unload material or products? Do you have two or three people sharing an office or not enough parking spaces? These are a few telltale signs that you need a larger facility. Your commercial facility should help your company make money, not hinder it due to a lack of workspace or functionality.

If you have hired a material handling specialist and utilized all their recommendations and are still tripping over yourself in the warehouse, then you need to entertain leasing a larger facility.

Question: If my company grows too large and my lease is still in force, can I end my lease or sublease the space?

Answer: The quick answer is yes. If you are located in California, then by California state law, you have the right to sublease your space with the written approval of the landlord. In almost all leases, there will be a paragraph or more on the terms and conditions of subleasing your space.

This is a good opportunity to bring in a commercial real estate broker because a broker will know how much your space is worth, how fast you will be able to sublease it, and where you can relocate. They can also undertake all negotiations with your existing landlord and your future sublessee.

Question: I am a tenant, and my business is decreasing. How do I get out of my lease payments?

Answer: If you have a signed lease, you are responsible for all of the lease payments until the expiration of the lease.

Almost all leases contain a clause allowing a tenant to sublease a space. This permits you to sublease the space with the landlord's permission, which cannot be unreasonably withheld.

Speak to a commercial real estate broker to determine how much the space you want to sublease is worth and how long it will take to sublease the space.

You should also apprise yourself of your responsibilities during the term of the sublease. Remember, when you sublease your space, you are not walking away from the lease; you are responsible for the property until your original lease has expired. Once a sublease has been signed, the sublessee remits sublease payments to you, and you, in turn, remit lease payments to your landlord.

If the company to which you are subleasing is much stronger financially than yours, you could try to convince your landlord to write a new lease with the sublessee directly, which would let you off the hook, as you would no longer be the lessee.

However, if you do need to sublease your space due to financial difficulty, don't be a stranger to your landlord. Keep an open line of communication with them. The worst thing you can do is avoid their calls because you are embarrassed that you are unable to make the lease payments. Almost all landlords will give you an opportunity to either pay missed lease payments, reduce your rent for a time, or sublease the space so they can continue to receive a monthly income from their property.

FINE-TUNING

Question: If I am looking to lease a space in a multi-tenant building or an industrial park, does it matter who the other tenants are or what their business is?

Answer: When you tour a commercial space, it's important to find out who your neighbors are. Are they competitors? If so, could they pose a threat to your business? For example, could they poach your customers? On the other hand, perhaps the neighbors could complement your business, which would make the new location more convenient for you and possibly save you time and money.

Once you sign a lease for three years, five years, or more, you are stuck with whatever businesses are nearby, so it's a good idea to get to know your neighbors beforehand.

Question: What are zoning and land-use areas? What do I need to know about them?

Answer: When it comes to zoning and land use, it's imperative that you ascertain not only that a property is properly zoned for the use you intend but also that the zoning of adjacent or nearby properties will not create conflicts. It's important to investigate land-use and zoning issues carefully so you are assured that your type of business, your manufacturing process, and your hours of operation are compliant with the zoning in which your building is located. A good method that I practice with my clients prior to signing a lease is to personally visit the zoning counter, confirm the zoning, confirm that the tenant's business is accepted in the specific zoned area, and procure a business license from the city that day.

Question: Should I have my attorney review the lease?

Answer: Yes, definitely, and be sure they are an experienced commercial real estate attorney. Some attorneys are great litigators, but I wouldn't want them negotiating or reviewing my lease. Attorneys specialize, just like most other professionals, so use the one best qualified to handle your real estate questions and concerns.

Your real estate broker can probably give you a couple of referrals. Be sure to have a telephone conversation with them before choosing one to represent you in any real estate matter. Remember the old cliché, "An ounce of prevention is worth a pound of cure"? A good professional real estate attorney is well worth the cost, as they can save you time, money, and headaches.

Question: I know that if I'm buying a building, I should have a certified inspector, but what about if I'm leasing a building? Should I use the services of a certified inspector as well?

Answer: A commercial building can be inspected by a certified commercial real estate inspector. This could cost less than $1,000 and often costs even less. So, it's money well invested.

Prior to signing a lease, a certified property inspector can alert you to items in need of repair or replacement that could cost you money over the term of your lease. If these items can be discovered and noted prior to signing the lease, there is a possibility that the landlord might repair or replace them before you take possession or give you a credit on the lease if you accept the property as is or complete the repairs yourself. If you don't want the item repaired or replaced, take note of it (including photos) so you are not responsible for it when you vacate the property.

A certified property inspector could also discover improvements to the property that may not have been built or installed to code. As a tenant, you might be held responsible for these modifications if there is an accident or if a government agency inspects the property and holds you liable for any repairs or replacements.

Quick Thought: *If you are leasing a building that has been previously occupied by a painting-use business, auto-use business, or any business that you think might have used chemicals, you might think about getting a Phase 1 environmental study completed. Not only can you use the results of the study for your own health protection, but you can also use it as a baseline for known pollution or environmental concerns. An added benefit is that you will not be blamed for the existing environmental problems if they arise in the future.*

©Marty Bucella   www.martybucella.com

"I suppose you're right. Some extra fire coverage would be a no-brainer."

Question: Who pays for insurance, and what type of insurance do I need as a tenant?

Answer: There are many different types of insurance; however, depending on the lease, the main types of insurance a tenant is required to obtain are property insurance in case of fire or destruction and liability insurance in the event someone hurts themselves in or around the property.

Regardless of the type of lease, all tenants need to obtain liability insurance. The lease is usually specific as to the minimum amount of liability insurance the tenant must obtain. The tenant must also name the landlord as an additional insured on the liability insurance. Once liability insurance is obtained by the tenant, proof of insurance must be shown to the landlord before the tenant will be allowed to occupy the facility.

Liability is generally the only type of insurance a tenant is required to obtain in a gross lease. In a net lease, the tenant will also be required to obtain property insurance in case of fire or destruction. Typically, a lease will call for you to show the landlord proof of any insurance you purchase.

If a tenant forgets to purchase the proper insurance and, consequently, doesn't show proof of insurance to the landlord, the landlord can purchase the insurance for the tenant and charge them for the cost of obtaining the insurance, as per the lease. In gross leases, more often than not, the landlord will pay for the property insurance, and the cost will be included in the tenant's monthly lease payment.

Also worth noting, any increase in property insurance premiums due to the nature of the tenant's business will be paid for by the tenant. For example, a chemical business will incur premium rates for fire insurance; that increase in premiums will be borne by the tenant.

Furthermore, in a gross lease, if, upon renewal of the insurance, the premiums increase, that increase is passed on to the tenant.

Question: What is a percentage lease?

Answer: Under a percentage lease, a tenant pays a base rent plus a percentage of any revenue earned while doing business on the rental premises. This is most commonly used in retail commercial property.

Sometimes a percentage lease agreement will decrease the base rent a lessee pays but give the landlord an increased percentage of the income the business makes. A percentage lease may offer the landlord additional potential as the revenue of that business increases.

Question: What are usable square feet and rentable square feet, and what's the difference?

Answer: Usable square footage comprises the office space, kitchen/break rooms, and private restrooms of your office suite. Rentable square footage includes the usable space plus the common areas of the building, such as hallways, lobbies, restrooms, etc. This terminology is usually used when describing pure office buildings with multiple tenants.

Quick Thought: Most commercial property is advertised as "approximately so many square feet." Measure out the space. If the amount you measure is larger than advertised, remain silent. If it's less, bring it to the landlord's attention!

Question: How much insurance will I need?

Answer: The type of lease you are entering into will determine how much insurance you need. But you can always purchase more insurance depending on how well protected you want to be.

If you are entering into a net lease, you will have to purchase or reimburse the landlord for fire insurance or insurance that covers damage or destruction to the building resulting from any type of destruction. Regardless of whether you enter into a net lease or a gross lease, you will also be required to purchase liability insurance in the amount indicated in the lease document. It's always a good idea to include your insurance agent in your decision-making process.

Random Question:

Have you ever done a real estate deal with a famous person or a movie star?

Answer: Working in Southern California with the Angels, Dodgers, Rams, Chargers, Lakers, and Clippers around; movie and television celebrities everywhere; and famous heads of businesses nearby, it isn't uncommon to bump into a famous name while working in the commercial real estate business. I have had the good fortune to work with people we would all recognize, but I treat my commercial real estate business much like an attorney and never disclose whom I am working with, what I am working on, the price paid, or the specifics of the transaction. All of my clients deserve and receive the same treatment: discretion, privacy, and confidentiality. Do you hear that, TMZ?

(Thanks, Madonna!)

Question: I have an option to renew my lease but no specific price. The lease states "current market rent or price." What is the definition of market rent or market price?

Answer: Market price is what the majority of buyers and sellers or landlords and tenants have agreed to. You can obtain actual sales prices for commercial real estate after the sale has occurred at the county assessor's office, as these are public records. By assembling a list of properties that have sold in a particular area, you can determine what the market price is for a particular property.

Market rent can be determined by obtaining the actual deal points for various similar leased properties in a particular area. Since these are not public records, and the details are only known by the landlords, tenants, and commercial real estate brokers who were involved in the transactions, this is more difficult to ascertain.

If you have a very good commercial real estate broker, they will be able to obtain comparable market rent data for leased properties in order to determine which way the market is headed and/or the current market rent.

With this information in hand, a tenant can better understand what is happening in the market and can tailor their lease renewal offer so that they don't pay more than the market rent. This can save the tenant thousands of dollars over the lifetime of the lease.

Question: How can I be more confident about the property I am interested in leasing? Is there a way to help verify some of the information I've been told?

Answer: You or your broker should have a checklist of items that are important to you when leasing a commercial facility. You can put together your own list or consider using the American Industrial Real Estate (AIR) Association's Property Information Sheet, which is very often used in the sale of industrial property but not as often in leasing industrial property. The two-page document can be given to the landlord for completion. The Property Information Sheet covers questions about equipment on the property, utilities, hazardous substances or mold, as well as any past leases or options, etc. Additionally, you can also employ the services of a professional property inspector.

Question: Am I able to sublease a portion or all of my facility? My landlord doesn't allow some uses.

Answer: Let's address any landlords who don't allow subleases. Sorry, landlords, but California state law states that all lessees have the right to sublease. However, a landlord still has the right to refuse a sublease based upon the sublessee's financials and type of business, among other things.

For example, if the sublessee's financials are not as strong as the original lessee's or there is a concern about the sublessee's financials, the landlord can reject the sublessee for those reasons. Furthermore, if the sublessee's type of business is one that might not be compatible with adjacent tenants, does not comply with the zoning ordinances, might be destructive to the building, or might give rise to an environmental concern, the landlord can refuse to sublease on that basis. But generally speaking, financials and business uses can be investigated, and if acceptable, the landlord will most often grant the sublease. (I bet you have never read a paragraph with the word "sublessee" used so often.)

Question: I want to sublease my building, but the owner says I can't. What now?

Answer: As stated in the previous answer, California state law provides for subleasing a facility as long as the owner approves of it in writing. The landlord's approval cannot be unreasonably withheld. However, there are certain ways a landlord can discourage their tenant from subleasing.

One of the most popular ways that is often included in commercial leases is to stipulate that any increase in the rental income paid by the sublessee to the lessee shall go to the landlord. This deters a tenant from subleasing their space in an effort to gain an incremental profit, especially in an upward-moving market. If you decide that you would like to sublease your space, hire the best commercial real estate agent to help you navigate this tricky process and determine the possible financial outcome.

Subleases are tricky, as they involve three separate parties (lessor, lessee, and sublessee), and all of them have to agree.

Question: What if I want an option to purchase the property during my lease?

Answer: If you are entering into a lease as a tenant and eventually want to become a property owner yourself, you might want to negotiate an option to purchase the property during the term of your lease.

When considering this, you should consult a real estate broker to determine what the property value might be in the future. Is it a rising market? Is it a declining market? Is a recession around the corner? Will the good times continue? How does the property in this location compare with properties in other locations? These are all factors to consider when making this decision.

A property will usually be worth more in the future than it is now. So, you will be very hard pressed to find a landlord who will give you an option to purchase a property at the same terms two, three, four, or five years from now.

If you are lucky enough to obtain an option to purchase the property, you might expect an increase in the purchase price as the years go by. And why not have part of your rent go toward the purchase price? You can ask, but in my entire career, I've rarely seen this happen. It's something that would be nice but hardly ever occurs.

If the landlord will not accept an option to purchase, try for a first right of refusal to purchase the property.

Question: What is the first right of refusal (right of first refusal)?

Answer: If an owner is leasing a building to a tenant, the tenant has asked to purchase the building, but the owner does not want to sell the property, then the first right of refusal is something the owner might grant the tenant. With a first right of refusal, the tenant has the opportunity to purchase the property should the property owner decide to sell it in the future. It can typically work in one of two ways.

Scenario 1: You, the tenant, have signed a five-year lease. During the term of the lease, the property owner decides to sell the property. The owner must approach you before anyone else and ask if you would like to purchase the property. You will then have a limited amount of time to communicate your decision back to the property owner. Should you decide to purchase the property, you can execute a purchase agreement, enter into escrow, and, if all goes well, you will own the property that you once leased.

Scenario 2: During the term of your lease, a third party makes an offer to the property owner to purchase the property. Before responding to the third-party offer, the owner must approach you, the tenant, with a bona fide offer from the third party and ask if you would like to meet the terms offered by the third party—hence the term "right of first refusal." If you agree, the property owner must offer and sell the property to you.

Question: What is the difference between an option and a first right of refusal?

Answer: An option to renew a lease or purchase a property is given to a tenant by a landlord. The tenant has the option to renew the lease or purchase the property at a future point in time.

The first right of refusal, or a right of first refusal in a real estate contract, is typically a mechanism that gives a specific party the right to be the first to purchase a particular property if it's offered for sale. The holder of a first right of refusal has the right to refuse to buy the property.

The right of first refusal is usually triggered when a third party offers to buy or lease a property from the owner. Before the property owner can accept the offer from the third party, the person with the right of first refusal (the existing tenant) must be given the opportunity to buy or lease the asset under the same terms offered by the third party.

Question: What is an option to cancel a lease, and how does it work?

Answer: An option to cancel the lease can vary depending on a multitude of factors. Most options to cancel a lease are for the tenant's benefit. Basically, once a tenant leases a facility, they will eventually decide whether the location and business plan work for the company. If they do, then the lease continues. If they do not, then the company has the option to cancel the lease. However, an option to cancel a lease is very rare because most landlords won't want to cancel a lease once they have a good, financially sound tenant.

Landlords also won't want to cancel a lease unless they receive some sort of reimbursement. Many landlords will ask for a buyout or a cash advance for canceling the lease, which will typically amount to three to six months of lease payments.

So, if the lease rate is $6,000 per month and the landlord requires you to pay six months of lease payments in order to cancel the lease, you can expect to pay $36,000 to walk away from your lease obligation. Lease cancellations occur very seldom, but they can be a good escape valve for a company that chooses this option over subleasing the space to a third party.

Question: What happens if the landlord fails to perform a covenant or requirement in the lease, such as a repair or maintenance?

Answer: Failure to perform a covenant or a requirement is known as a breach by the lessor. For example, if the lessor doesn't carry out a repair or fulfill a requirement indicated in the lease, the lessee/tenant shall notify the lessor/landlord in writing of the issue that needs to be repaired or remediated. If the landlord hasn't completed the repair or requirement thirty days from the date of the tenant's notice, the tenant may repair or remediate the issue at their own expense and offset the cost from their rent, provided the offset does not exceed an amount equal to one month's base rent. The tenant needs to document the cost and supply the documentation to the landlord.

It really comes down to your relationship and the communication you have with your lessor. I have found that the better the relationship and communication between lessor and lessee, the easier things go in terms of repairs and other items concerning the lease.

Question: The lease has an arbitration clause. What is that?

Answer: Many contracts these days include arbitration clauses. An arbitration clause states that both parties agree to settle any disputes through arbitration (a formal discussion before a moderator, typically a retired judge) rather than costly and time-consuming litigation. Read the lease contract to see if the arbitration clause is mandatory. Make sure you have the right to participate in selecting the arbitrator and other decisions regarding arbitration.

CLOSING

Question: I have signed the lease. When do I get the keys?

Answer: Just signing a lease does not get you access to the facility. There are at least, two additional hurdles you must clear before you can have access to your new facility:

- paying the first month's rent, security deposit, and any other costs associated with the monthly rent
- obtaining liability insurance for the property and naming the landlord as an additional insured

When you sign the lease, be sure to give the landlord a cashier's check that covers all of the funds required for you to move in. This way, the landlord doesn't have to wait for the check to clear before giving you the keys. The landlord also won't release the keys to the new tenant until the tenant obtains liability insurance. A landlord holding on to the keys and not giving access to the tenant is great leverage in getting these requirements completed.

As a tenant, make sure signing the lease, obtaining proper insurance, and having a cashier's check occur at the same time.

Question: After the lease expires and I move out, when will my security deposit be returned?

Answer: This can vary depending on the type of lease you entered into. The return of the security deposit should be mentioned in the lease and can range anywhere from thirty to ninety days, depending on the lease.

Within ninety days of the expiration or termination of the lease, the lessor shall return the portion of the security deposit not used or applied by the lessor. No part of the security deposit shall be held in an interest-bearing account in favor of the lessee.

There is often a mistaken belief that the security deposit is the last month's rent. It isn't the last month's rent. If the tenant has kept the building damage-free with the exception of ordinary wear and tear, there is no reason the tenant should not receive 100% of the security deposit back from the landlord. The security deposit is not a fund for the landlord to clean carpets and repaint the building. The security deposit is meant to guard against the tenant damaging the premises in excess of ordinary wear and tear.

Question: What is a personal guarantee? Do I have to sign a personal guarantee to lease commercial space?

Answer: A personal guarantee of the lease is a promise from a guarantor (typically the owner of the business leasing the property or the lessee) that in the event of a breach of the lease, the guarantor (lessee) will make good on the lessee's promises. For example, if the tenant fails to make rent, the landlord can sue the tenant to collect the rent.

A landlord might be a little hesitant to rent to a company with little business history, such as a startup, or even a more seasoned company. So, the landlord will ask for additional language in the lease to ensure they get their rent. This comes in the form of a personal guarantee.

So, how does it work? Do you have to sign one? Can you get out of signing one? Essentially, a personal guarantee in a commercial lease is pretty much what it sounds like; it makes you personally liable for the rent if your business can't pay. Considering the failure rate of new businesses, it's an obvious protection for landlords but offers a small business owner nothing in the way of financial or legal protection.

More and more commercial landlords are insisting upon personal guarantees from tenants, and most landlords will not sign a lease unless you personally guarantee it. So, consider yourself extremely lucky if you can get away with signing a lease without such a clause.

One way around a personal guarantee is to try and negotiate a release date for the guarantee with the landlord. If the lessor sees that you have been paying the rent on a consistent basis over a period of time, you can make a good case for removing a personal guarantee on your lease.

Another way to possibly avoid a personal guarantee from the outset is to convince the landlord that your company is financially healthy by providing them with your financial statements. Increasing the amount of your security deposit might also help you avoid signing a personal guarantee.

Expanding on the personal guarantee

A personal guarantee is a component of a lease contract or sometimes an entirely separate contract whereby an individual person agrees to be personally liable for the contract. In the event that their company breaches the contract, the landlord can pursue not only the tenant's assets but also the individual personal guarantor's assets, including their home, bank account, wages, investments, etc. So, be careful.

Question: The lease document is very long and not very interesting. Do I really need to know everything in it?

Answer: First, there are numerous items in a lease because it has to cover just about any situation that can arise during the lease term. Second, and most importantly, you should ensure that all the business points you negotiated are included in the lease, along with the obvious: the start date, end date, lease rate, options, etc. Make sure you know and understand what you are obligated to do and what the landlord is obligated to do.

Years ago, leases had less language and were less voluminous than the typical lease is now. Throughout the years, as difficult situations arose, fixes were added to successive leases to meet and address those needs. Even in my career of thirty-plus years, I have seen pages added to the basic lease, extending it from a nine-page document to more than fifteen pages. Some of the added items include hazardous substances, environmental situations, etc. One of the best ways to properly understand the complexities of a lease is to go through it paragraph by paragraph, if possible, with someone who understands it. This could be an experienced commercial real estate broker or a real estate attorney.

True Story

You would think that if you were a Fortune 500 company, you could just about lease any facility you wanted, and any landlord would welcome such a well-known, well-financed company. Not the landlord I represented.

This landlord demanded a personal guarantee from a Fortune 500 company. The Fortune 500 company had never done this before and protested, but the landlord stood firm. Since the company really needed that particular location for its business, three company officers actually signed the personal guarantee. Needless to say, the Fortune 500 company never missed a rent payment.

DEFINITIONS YOU NEED TO KNOW

Initially, I didn't want to include a section on definitions because I thought that would make this book seem too much like a textbook. However, I thought I would add some words and phrases that are used every day in the commercial real estate brokerage business but may not be understood by those who do not work in the industry. So, here you go: my top ninety definitions.

Accretion, Alluvium, & Avulsion: Three terms whose sole purpose is to confuse you on state real estate exams and whose definitions you will only remember until the test is over.

Adjoining: In actual contact with another object (i.e., attached). Means the same as "contiguous."

Amps: Amps are simply the amount of electricity used by an item. Volts are a measure of the strength of electricity. Amps multiplied by volts gives you the total wattage (workload or working capacity of the electricity). Understanding how the three terms relate will help you understand the electrical requirements of an item. Wanna call an electrician yet?

Anchor Tenant: The primary and usually the largest tenant in a shopping center. Larger shopping centers may have more than one anchor tenant. Rent for anchor tenants is often significantly lower per square foot than rent for other tenants in the shopping center because they drive consumers to the center.

Apron: No, not the kind that June Cleaver wore. This apron is the area within a truck court where trucks are parked for loading and unloading. This area is usually paved with a more durable material such as concrete to withstand the heavy loads resulting from the staging and parking of trucks.

Bay Depth: The distance between columns.

Bay Width: The distance from one side of the bay columns to the other.

Blend and Extend: A blend and extend lease is a type of renewal that allows tenants to blend their existing lease with a new and longer lease. If a tenant is paying rent that is above current market rents, this arrangement will lower the current rental rate. The tenant benefits from an immediate reduction in the rental rate, and the landlord benefits by securing a tenant for a longer term. Alternatively, if the rent is rising quickly and lease expiration is approaching, a tenant may renew early and extend to lock in lower rates.

Block Building: A building that is constructed from brick or masonry blocks instead of steel or concrete tilt-up.

Build-Out: Improvements to the interior of a space, including flooring, walls, finished plumbing, electrical work, etc.

Build to Suit: Designing and tailoring a building for a specific tenant, often because the tenant is unable to find a suitable space in the speculative market.

Calculated Sprinkler

System: A fire sprinkler system within a building that has been set to have a particular water flow rate pass through a fire sprinkler system during a set time. (For example, 0.45 GPM means 0.45 gallons will flow through a sprinkler head in one minute's time.)

Capitalization Rate

or Cap Rate: Unlevered initial return from the acquisition of a real estate asset, calculated by dividing the operating income by the property's sale price. For example, a property's capitalization rate (cap rate) is 10% of the purchase if it was purchased for $10 million and produced $1 million in net operating income in one year. The cap rate is typically calculated using the net operating income generated in the first year of ownership so investors can compare potential returns on comparable investment properties.

Clear Height: Distance from the floor to the lowest hanging ceiling member or hanging objects such as beams, joists, or truss work descending into a substantial portion of the industrial work area. This is the most important measure of the interior height of an industrial building because it defines the minimum height of usable space within the structure.

Clear Span

Warehouse: An open area with no obstructions, such as support poles.

Cold Storage

Warehouse: A storage warehouse used to store fresh and/or frozen perishable items including, but not limited to, fruits or vegetables, meat, seafood, dairy products, or medicines at a desired temperature to maintain the quality of the product for orderly marketing.

General temperatures:

Refrigeration: 33 to 55 degrees Fahrenheit

Freezer: 14 to 18 degrees Fahrenheit

Low Freezer: -10 to -20 degrees Fahrenheit

Column Spacing: The distance between support posts in a building.

Commercial Real Estate: Property that is used exclusively for business-related purposes or to provide a workspace rather than a living space, which would instead constitute residential real estate. Commercial real estate is usually leased to tenants to conduct income-generating activities.

Concessions: To secure a tenant when the vacancy rate is high in the market, a landlord may need to grant concessions in the lease. These concessions most often take the form of free rent but may also include lease buyouts and above-market tenant improvement allowances.

Conditional Use Permit (CUP): Allows a city or county to consider special uses that may be essential or desirable to a particular community but are not allowed as a matter of right within a zoning district. This is accomplished through a public hearing process.

Contingency: A requirement in a contract that must occur before that contract can be finalized.

Creative Office Space: Previously industrial space with high ceilings and exposed air ducts. The space is often made of brick and timber and has been converted to office or studio space that often caters to technology, advertising, media, and entertainment tenants.

Cross Dock: Loading docks on opposite sides of a relatively shallow distribution facility that allow for quick loading, sorting, or unloading from one vehicle to another. (Materials from one truck at a loading dock are unloaded, sorted, and reloaded onto one or more trucks.)

Distribution Building: A type of warehouse facility designed to accommodate efficient movement of goods. Typically, these buildings have high clearance, wide column spacing, and many truck doors to facilitate the warehousing and distribution of goods.

Dock High Door: A loading dock door that isn't at ground level but is instead elevated to four feet in order to be even with the standard tractor-trailer height for loading or unloading goods without a change in elevation.

Electrical Distribution: The spreading of electricity from the main power panel to different locations throughout a building to make it convenient to plug in machines and equipment.

ESFR Fire Sprinklers: Early suppression fast response (ESFR) systems are quick-responding, high-volume sprinkler systems that provide exceptional protection for high-piled storage occupancies. ESFR sprinklers are designed to release two to three times the amount of water of conventional sprinkler heads and emit larger droplets of water, which, in turn, have greater momentum than droplets emitted from conventional heads.

Estoppel Certificate: A document that verifies the major points (e.g., base rent, lease commencement, and lease expiration) of the existing lease between the landlord and tenant. An estoppel certificate might be utilized by the owner of the property to verify the existing leases of the property to a lending institution so as to help with support information for obtaining a loan.

Every Question Answered: If you want answers to questions, this is one of the best desktop reference books on commercial real estate that you can have in your possession.

Exclusive Agency: An agreement in which one broker has exclusive rights to represent the owner or tenant.

Fenced Yard Area: Come on, really?

Fiduciary: A person who represents another person on financial/property matters with the utmost care and integrity.

Fixtures: Personal property so attached to the land or building it's considered part of the real property. An example might be electrical distribution lines in a manufacturing building.

Free Span: A roof that spans from wall to wall without interior columns or pillars. Sometimes called a bow roof.

Functional Obsolescence: A descriptive term used to characterize a building that cannot be improved to meet current market standards or tastes without a complete replacement of buildings systems and finishes. An example might be small loading doors, small restrooms, or low ceiling height.

Gross Lease: A legally binding contract in which the landlord receives stipulated rent from a tenant and the landlord is obligated to pay all or most of the property's operating expenses and real estate taxes.

Ground Lease: A lease agreement whereby the landowner (lessor) agrees to lease a parcel of land for a set period of time to a lessee. Depending on the agreement, the lessor can stipulate what the lessee can or cannot do with (or build on) the property. The lease term can be for any number of years. It's typically for twenty years or more, but many extend it to ninety-nine years.

Upon expiration of the lease agreement, the lessor typically gains control and ownership of whatever is constructed on the land, unless the lease is renewed or an exception is created in the ground lease. Doesn't that sound like instructions for the Monopoly board game?

Ground-Level Loading Door: A door through which trucks, forklifts, and other vehicles or machinery can enter or exit a warehouse without a change in elevation. Also referred to as an overhead door.

Glulam Beam: A glulam beam is a stress-rated engineered wood beam composed of wood laminations or "lams" that are bonded (glued) together with durable, moisture-resistant adhesives.

GPM:	Gallons per minute. Also known as "flow rate," GPM is a measure of how many gallons of water flow out of a sprinkler head each minute. For example, a fire sprinkler head rated at 0.33 GPM means that about one-third of a gallon will flow through that particular fire sprinkler head per minute when activated.
High Cube:	Refers to industrial buildings with an abundance of clear height or vertical cubic space.
Holdover Tenant:	A tenant who remains in possession of leased property after the lease term's expiration.
Industrial Building:	A structure used primarily for manufacturing, research and development, production, maintenance, and storage and/or distribution of goods. You can include some office space in that definition. Industrial buildings are divided into three primary classifications: manufacturing, warehouse and distribution, and flex (research and development).
Infill:	Infill is the development of one or more buildings on underused land situated between existing buildings. Infill development is typically done in dense environments where land is scarce.
Insulation:	A material usually installed on the ceiling of an industrial building to act as a radiant barrier against the sun in order to keep the inside of a warehouse cooler. The material most commonly used is foil, which can be used exclusively or paired with fiberglass or foam.
Irrevocable:	Incapable of being altered, changed, or recalled.

Lessee: An individual or entity to whom property is rented under a lease (a tenant).

Lessor: An individual or entity who rents property to a tenant under a lease (a landlord).

Letter of Intent: Often referred to as an LOI, a letter of intent is a document outlining the intentions of two or more parties to do business together; it's often nonbinding, unless the language in the document specifies that the companies are legally bound by the terms.

Leveler: Steel plates that are sometimes moved by auto-hydraulic lifts to make a loading dock level with a truck bed. A fully loaded truck may sit four to six inches higher or lower than the standard forty-eight-inch-high dock. A leveler is used to account for the difference in height so a forklift can be easily driven into and out of a truck while loading.

Listing: An employment contract between a principal and an agent that authorizes the agent (such as a broker) to perform services for the principal and their property.

Loading Dock: An elevated platform at the shipping or delivery door of the building; it's usually situated at the same height as the floor of the shipping container on a truck or railroad car to facilitate loading and unloading. Loading docks can be exterior ramps that protrude from a building that are sometimes covered with a canopy to protect the loading area from the elements. Otherwise, they can be flush with the exterior of the building and accessed through a sliding door that is adjacent to the interior of the building.

Man Door: A standard-sized, walk-through door that enables you to enter the warehouse of an industrial building without the need to open a larger loading door. Maybe in this day and age, it should be called a person door.

Market Price: The actual selling price or leasing price of a property.

Market Value: The expected price that a property should bring if exposed for lease or sale on the open market for a reasonable period of time with market-savvy landlords and tenants or sellers and buyers.

Master Lease: The original, primary, and controlling lease between the original lessor and lessee identifying the terms and length of the original lease. Note that a sublease cannot extend beyond the original term of a master lease.

Medical Office Building: A structure with at least 75% of its interior built out to accommodate healthcare providers such as doctors or dentists or healthcare technicians. Ordinarily, these buildings have more robust mechanical, electrical, and plumbing systems. Such buildings will also have more parking spaces to accommodate their increased parking needs.

Multiple Listing Service (MLS): No, this is not the abbreviation for major league soccer. This is a generic title for more than two-dozen listing services of commercial property throughout the nation. If you are only looking at one or two of these services, you are not seeing the whole picture.

Multi-Tenant Building: A building that isn't typically owner-occupied, with space that is leased to two or more tenants.

Net Cash Flow: Net cash flow is the annual income produced by an investment property after deducting allowances for capital repairs, leasing commissions, tenant inducements, and the debt service from net operating income.

Net Lease: A lease in which the tenant pays their share of operating expenses in addition to the stipulated rent. Disclosure to the tenant of the specific expenses to be paid directly by the tenant is required.

Net Operating Income (NOI): Net operating income is the income generated after deducting operating expenses but before deducting taxes and financing expenses. If this is starting to hurt your head, call a CPA.

Option to Extend or Renew (Lease): The right of a tenant to extend the lease term for a specified period of time at a predefined rental rate. The rate is frequently defined as a percentage of market rent, but sometimes the rate is a specified dollar amount. There is usually a date by which this option must be exercised; otherwise, it may expire.

Option to Purchase: An option to purchase real estate is a legally binding contract that allows a prospective buyer to enter into an agreement with a seller in which the buyer is given the exclusive option to purchase the property for a period of time and for a certain (sometimes variable) price.

In most instances, an option to purchase can be included in a lease agreement whereby a tenant signs a lease that also grants them the opportunity to purchase the property.

The purchase price can be fixed—a price that the potential buyer and property owner have agreed to in advance—or it can be a variable price. When a lease agreement extends over a period of years, the purchase price may be adjusted for inflation and/or based on a new appraisal at that time.

Power Panel: The electrical power panel is the connection between the external wires coming from the street and the internal wires of the building's electrical system. Also known as "that big gray box in the corner of the building." Try finding these boxes in any color other than gray.

Rail Door: A loading door that is generally side loading, has access to railroad tracks, and facilitates the loading or unloading of goods from a railroad car to an industrial building.

Rail Service: A railroad spur adjacent to a building structure that allows the building to be served by rail operations.

Ramp Door: A dock-high door that has been converted to a drive-in door by creating a ramp from the ground level to the dock level.

Service Center or Showroom: A type of flex facility characterized by a substantial showroom area. Usually fronting a freeway or major road.

Shell Space: Space within a building that is currently not built out.

Short Sale: A sale in which the sale price of an asset is less than the amount owed to the lender, and the lender accepts this as full payment for the loan.

Skylight: A light-transmitting structure that takes up a portion of the roof space of a building and is designed to let more light into the building in the daylight hours.

Space Heater: A large, box-like machine in an industrial building, most often hung from the ceiling, that heats up the interior of the building in colder weather. Most often, these space heaters run on natural gas.

Square Feet: The useful method by which building space is defined. The area is calculated by multiplying the length by the width. For example, a twenty-foot by forty-foot room has an area of eight hundred square feet.

Staging Area: Exterior area adjacent to an industrial building's loading docks or doors where trucks maneuver. The most important measurement of a truck court is the depth from the building to the end of the truck court. Greater depth allows for greater maneuverability and better accommodates multiple trucks.

Daniel

Tenants in Common: An estate held by two or more persons, each of whom has an undivided interest, which means that each party has the right to sell or transfer their ownership interest.

Tenant Improvements: Work done on the interior of a space, which can be paid for by the landlord, tenant, or some combination of both, depending on the terms of the lease.

Third-Party Logistics: Businesses that provide one or more logistics services, including multiclient warehousing, contract warehousing, transportation management, distribution management, inventory management, and freight consolidation.

Tilt-Up Building or Construction: Tilt-up construction or concrete tilt-up gets its name from the manner in which the construction occurs: by lifting or tilting concrete panels with a crane to form the walls of a building. Basically, the floor of the building is poured concrete, and once it dries, portions of the walls are poured onto the dried concrete floor. Once the concrete walls are dry, they are lifted and tilted around the perimeter of the floor to form the building. The process is interesting and fun to watch.

Triple Net Lease: This is much the same as a net lease. Many net leases are triple net leases because in addition to the rent (or net rent), the tenant is financially responsible for the big three expenses: taxes, insurance, and maintenance. Generally, the tenant is responsible for all the expenses regarding the leased property, while the landlord is responsible for the roof, the structure itself, and sometimes the parking lot.

Truck Turning Radius: The tightest turn a truck can make. This depends on several variables, such as truck configuration, trailer size, and the location of adjacent objects that obstruct the inner turning radius.

Truck Well: A truck well is commonly used to provide dock-high loading for a grade-level warehouse. A well is dug about four feet below ground level so a truck can back in and load. It's important that a truck well be long enough so that when the truck is in the well, there is only a slight incline; you don't want the contents of the truck to move or tip over.

There are some possible disadvantages: it requires more land to maneuver large trucks as they approach the well; wells could require pumps to evacuate water after it rains; and shorter truck wells mean that trucks could be sloping downward after parking at the dock, which is problematic for some loads.

Truss: A framework of beams forming a rigid structure, as in a roof truss.

Truss Height: The distance from the floor to the bottom edge of a truss used to support the ceiling or roof of a building. If there are hanging objects, beams, or joists below the truss, the clear height will be lower than the truss height.

Turnkey: Literally means that once the building is completed, you can turn the key in the front door and start using it immediately. No further work is required, as the building is ready for immediate use.

Vacancy Rate: The vacancy rate is the percentage of all the square footage of a rental space that is vacant in relation to the total amount of existing square footage. The formula to calculate the vacancy rate is the available square feet divided by the total existing square feet.

Value Added: An investment in a real estate asset with existing cash flow that can be increased by raising occupancy, rents, or both. Owners typically carry out one or more of the following to add value to a building: improve or replace building systems, provide new finishes, introduce new amenities, improve access or circulation to the building, add square footage, etc.

Void: Something that is unenforceable.

Voidable: A situation that is capable of being unenforceable but isn't unless direct action is taken.

Zoning Ordinance: A law by a local government authority, such as a city or county, that sets the parameters by which the property may be used. (I needed a word with Z. It looks bad if a list of definitions ends with a V-word and not a Z-word.)

About the Author

DAN KRUSE has been an industrial real estate agent since 1982, when he graduated from California State University, Fullerton, with a BA in business finance with an emphasis on real estate finance. Dan also received a certificate in marketing from the Wharton Business School, University of Pennsylvania.

Beginning his career at Grubb & Ellis and Schneider Commercial Real Estate, Dan received numerous awards for being a top producer before eventually joining forces with Lee & Associates Commercial Real Estate Services, where he has been a principal and owner for over twenty-eight years.

Born in Orange County, California, Dan had a variety of jobs growing up. He flipped burgers and made ice cream cones at Tastee-Freez, was a lifeguard at community swimming pools, worked at Knott's Berry Farm, and was a magician in the Magic Shop at Disneyland. (You don't get much more Orange County, California, than that.)

Dan is an active member of the American Industrial Real Estate Association (AIR), where he sits on the Advisory Council. Dan strongly supports various environmental organizations, including the World Wildlife Fund and the Arbor Day Foundation.

Dan can be contacted via his website at **www.DanielPKruse.com**.

About the Illustrator

The Artist

While passing time in college, **MARTY BUCELLA** designed a greeting card for his girlfriend (now his wife) and thought, "Hey, maybe I can make money doing this!" And he did . . . if you consider $30 money. The rest of his senior year in college was spent drawing in notebooks instead of taking notes.

Upon graduation, he had many rejections, but he picked himself up and started doing single-panel gag cartoons. His first sales (a batch of four) went for $5 each to a publication called *Glass Digest*. The rest, as they say, is history.

Marty has sold tens of thousands of cartoons, humorous illustrations, greeting cards, ads, etc. and has been published in more than five hundred markets, including magazines, calendars, greeting cards, newspapers, ads, books, and more. Some of these markets include Macy's, *Better Homes & Gardens*, *The Wall Street Journal*, *The National Enquirer*, King Features Syndicate, *The Saturday Evening Post*, *Chicken Soup for the Soul*, *Woman's World*, Apple Computer, *Reader's Digest*, *Good Housekeeping*, Paramount Cards, *Family Circle*, McGraw-Hill, etc.

Marty is pleased to be included in Dan's *Every Question Answered*.

Marty hopes to continue until he drops dead or wins the lottery . . . whichever comes first.

www.ingramcontent.com/pod-product-compliance
Lightning Source LLC
Chambersburg PA
CBHW041510120626
46551CB00018B/2376

9798988210009